More advance praise for *The Career T*

"Taguchi offers wonderfully structured and well thought-out practical advice. She has an enormous passion and gift for inspiring and helping others make the most of their careers and figure out how to live their best work lives. Our jobs are major factors in determining our happiness in life, and this book addresses many of the career challenges that most everyone will face either now or in the future. The straight-up advice, caring style, and actionable strategies and steps make The Career Troubleshooter *an easy and enjoyable read."*

—Simon Sutton, Executive Vice President, International Television, Metro-Goldwyn-Mayer, Inc.

"I like the way the book covers the variety of challenges I and so many of my friends are facing now or will face during the course of our careers . . . challenges such as what's next, coming back from a career break, dealing with a bad boss or difficult colleagues, deserving a raise or promotion, dealing with a dead-end career path. These are all very real issues for us today, and the practical, straightforward strategies, advice, and steps to take are not only incredibly helpful, but give a sense of empowerment in how to take positive steps toward resolution."

—Carol Ramos, Senior Manager, Yahoo Finance

"As someone who has led MBA recruiting and hired/managed a wide range of talented people, I've seen those who can overcome career or work-related challenges before they turn into out-of-control problems, and those who don't have a clue. This book offers relevant, timely, and incredibly helpful advice for 21 of the most common career challenges. Taguchi shares what you need to do to thrive through the challenges while strengthening your career and satisfaction with work."

—Andrew D. Miller, VP Corporate Controller, Autodesk, Inc.

"I have seen Sherrie Taguchi in action. She has an amazing ability to teach and inspire others. Her own depth of experience in industry and education, her natural generosity of heart, and her positive energy imbue and inform her work. I particularly admire how Sherrie

can help people from all kinds of backgrounds figure out how to take steps to make their work lives the most fulfilling possible."
> —Deanna Mulligan, Former Executive Vice President, AXA Financial

"If you want to have your best career, this book is an incredible resource. Taguchi gives you real-world solutions, creative ideas, and a wealth of tips and tools. I'd recommend it for all students to get a head start on how to sidestep common work challenges; for professionals who want to take action on building a meaningful and successful career; for managers who want to coach their employees through their challenges; and for career development professionals who are advising their students on career management for a lifetime."
> —Dr. Karen O. Dowd, Senior Director of MBA Career Development, University of Notre Dame, Mendoza College of Business

"This book lets you play at the top your game. It gives you winning strategies, the right moves, and great coaching."
> —Jason Smith, Director, Strategic Relationship Marketing, VeriSign, Inc.

"Illuminating and inspiring! Sage advice for anyone wanting to come back from a career break. As a working mom who stepped off of a fast track career to have two children, then went on to start up a successful CPA and professional services firm, I applaud Sherrie Taguchi's accessible and actionable strategies and tips on everything you need to know to face the challenges of returning to work after time off or downshifting in your career. I hire and mentor many men and women who are grappling with work-family challenges. This book is a wealth of practical guidance. The useful exercises and resources that allow you to figure out what's next for your career and then what to do to get there are priceless."
> —Diana Chan, CEO, Chan CPA and Co.

THE CAREER TROUBLESHOOTER

Tips and Tools for Overcoming the 21 Most Common Challenges to Success

Sherrie Gong Taguchi

AMACOM

American Management Association

New York • Atlanta • Brussels • Chicago • Mexico City • San Francisco
Shanghai • Tokyo • Toronto • Washington, D.C.

This publication is designed to provide accurate and authoritative information in regard to the subject matter covered. It is sold with the understanding that the publisher is not engaged in rendering legal, accounting, or other professional service. If legal advice or other expert assistance is required, the services of a competent professional person should be sought.

Various names used by companies to distinguish their software and other products can be claimed as trademarks. AMACOM uses such names throughout this book for editorial purposes only, with no intention of trademark violation. All such software or product names are in initial capital letters or ALL CAPITAL letters. Individual companies should be contacted for complete information regarding trademarks and registration.

Library of Congress Cataloging-in-Publication Data

Taguchi, Sherrie Gong, 1961–
      The career troubleshooter : tips and tools for overcoming the 21 most common challenges to success / Sherrie Gong Taguchi.
          p.   cm.
      Includes index.
      ISBN 0-8144-7229-X (pbk.)
      1. Career development.   2. Job hunting.   3. Job security.   4. Career changes.   5. Managing your boss.   6. Problem employees.   I. Title.

HF5381.T2212   2006
331.702—dc22

                                                                                      2005011791

Printing number

10   9   8   7   6   5   4   3   2   1

To

Mark
you are the most loving and
supportive husband
and best friend

Magen
thank you for being an incredible mom and for
the gifts you share with me generously—your gorgeous heart
and amazing love, energy, and spirit

Contents

Acknowledgments

THIS BOOK would not have been possible without the involvement of literally hundreds of people. A heartfelt thanks to the following executives for their valuable insights or inspiration: Andrew Miller, Autodesk; Diana Chan, Chan CPA and Co.; Carol Escueta Ramos, eBay, Inc.; John Celona, Hewlett-Packard; Karen Yukawa, Honda International; Paul Reilly, Korn/Ferry International; Eric Snyder, Louis Vuitton Moët Hennessy, Inc.; William F. Meehan III, McKinsey and Company; Simon Sutton, Metro-Goldwyn-Mayer, Inc.; Jana Rich, Russell Reynolds Associates; Lance Choy, Stanford University; Rebecca Chopra, Stanford University Graduate School of Business; Dr. Karen O. Dowd, University of Notre Dame; Jaynee Meyer, University of Southern California; Jason Smith, VeriSign, Inc.

Special appreciation goes to Keith Wilson, of London, England, who created the graphic art and figures for this book.

I've a debt of gratitude to my talented editors, Ellen Kadin and Barry Richardson. Ellen, thank you for your commitment to making this book a reality. Your able shepherding of our project, energizing collaboration, and breadth of wisdom have been invaluable. Barry, you have been incredible with your focused edits to the manuscript and elegant insights. Erika Spelman and the production team, you were terrific in keeping the book on track and progressing smoothly. Cathleen Ouderkirk, thank you for your artistic excellence.

To the many wonderful people with whom I've worked—teams I have managed, clients, colleagues, managers, CEOs—you have taught me so much throughout the years, enlightening my work life and inspiring my continuous learning. To my early mentors at Bank of America—Jim Miscoll, Helene Young, Peggy Hiraoka, Bob Beck, and Bill Crozier—thank you for giving me so many opportunities to test myself and to build a strong base of experience at such a young age. Dick Lau and Wes Smith at Dole Packaged Foods were remarkable mentors who helped me shape my management philosophy to lead with my heart and my head, balancing compassion for people with business needs. Marge Holmes at Mervyn's was a great example of staying in touch with your values and being true to yourself in going for a bold, meaningful, and dynamic career, not a comfortable, cushy one. Mike Spence and George Parker of the Stanford Graduate School of Business—thank you for being such extraordinary leaders and managers. Your lessons on embracing an entrepreneurial spirit and being an eternal student are priceless. Jim Collins, one of my favorite professors while at the Stanford Business School, is the gold standard for someone living his purpose, passion, and path every day in his work. You are an audacious inspiration for doing what you love and loving what you do while touching people's lives.

Introduction

DURING MY 18 YEARS as a senior manager, recruiter, and career management author and adviser, working with thousands of students, professionals, and executives on their careers and workplace problems, one thing has become very clear. Many of us face the same career and workplace problems over our lifetime.

For me, it has been both gratifying and an integral part of my life's work to share what knowledge and experience I have to help, develop, teach, and inspire others in a variety of ways: recruiting top talent for my own teams or for managers who have hiring needs; advising mid- to senior-level managers on their own career dilemmas and turning points or on issues/problems with their employees; consulting to hundreds of companies on finding and keeping the best talent; and guiding individuals throughout the many stages of their careers on job searches and major career changes.

The rich and diverse experiences have been learning filled and rewarding. They have also given me a unique vantage point and "laboratory" for distilling and studying a core set of the most common challenges people face in their job searches, careers, and workplaces, and what works best to solve these challenges.

I am excited to share this book with you. It puts you in the driver's seat—empowers you to tackle the most common career challenges you'll face in your jobs, careers, and workplaces. This book discusses 21 top career challenges, with strategies, advice, and resources on how to solve them. These 21 common problems may be big and debilitating or small and frustrating; they have the potential to derail a career or keep you in a job that makes you unhappy. More often than not, the challenges make you feel stressed, overwhelmed, unconfident, or demoralized. They can develop into a full-blown crisis if not handled skillfully and quickly.

The good news is that most career challenges—like so many other challenges—can be met. The purpose of this book is to provide you with useful advice along with helpful resources and tools that you can apply in conjunction with your own smarts and determination. You can overcome the challenges. In fact, you can work through them in such a way that they are transformed into valuable opportunities, fresh starts, or best-case scenarios. If you are clear on what career challenges you are dealing with, are open to learning what you can do to solve the problem, and will take action to help yourself, you can succeed in overcoming most any of them.

This book is made up of 21 chapters, each examining one of the most common problems that people face in their job searches, careers, and workplaces. The challenges represent a wide range of career concerns. The typical person will face many, if not all, of them in the course of a lifetime of work.

The first set of chapters (1 through 5) deals with looking for a job, offering not just valuable information on doing a job search but also on aligning your personal values with your job search, creating a strong résumé, learning the ins and outs of interviewing, and recharging a job search that lasts way beyond what you originally expected.

The next group of chapters (6 through 13) concerns on-the-job challenges, such as starting a new job, working for a bad boss, dealing with difficult colleagues, managing a new group of people, asking for a raise or promotion, feeling inadequate at your job, having no career path, and coping with unethical conduct.

Chapters 14 through16 discuss three major career-altering challenges thrust upon you by your employer: when you are being fired or forced out, when you must deal with the aftermath of a merger or acquisition, and when you are laid off.

The final five chapters (17 through 21) have to do with career choices that you undertake: making a major career change, taking a career break, resequencing your career for family, trailing your spouse to a new location, and not being sure of your career purpose or path.

Each chapter includes two to three core sections for easiest and maximum take-away learning. The first part decodes the challenge: What is the challenge? What does it look and feel like, so you know if you are really experiencing it? The second section provides you with a solution set of specific strategies, advice, tips, and how to's. These strategies offer a broad, diverse range of actionable to-do's, things to think about, and questions to ask yourself in order to help you deal with the challenges most effectively. You can pick and choose from among the ideas offered to create the best solution set for you. If applicable, a third section gives you engaging and useful tools and resources to get you started on and guide you through what you need to do to meet the challenge.

One of the truly useful features of the book is the cross-referencing of ideas from one chapter to another. While each chapter should be read on its own, especially if you are in the throes of the specific challenge being discussed, you'll soon realize that many of the challenges—as well as their resolutions—overlap in certain ways. For example, the ideas presented on doing a job search can be used in regard to other challenges, such as surviving a layoff, making a major career change, or trailing your spouse to a new location. You'll find yourself going back and forth from section to section, building a powerful set of solutions that will help you face and overcome any of the 21 career challenges described here.

Doing a Job Search

HAVE YOU RECENTLY BEEN laid off and need to start looking for a new job? Have you been unhappy in your job for a while and are dreaming about making a change when the job market picks up again? Have you recently been divorced or widowed and need to go back to work to support your family? Have you recently moved to a new city to follow a spouse or partner and are starting a job search? Are you on the home stretch of getting your degree and eager to land a great job? Do you anticipate that you'll lose your job sometime in the next few months and want to get a head start on a job search?

● DEFINING THE CHALLENGE

Doing a job search can be daunting, overwhelming, and stressful for a variety of reasons. For instance, you may not know where and how to begin. You realize that there are a lot of talented people looking for work, some even overqualified, vying for the same jobs you'll be trying for. This is a buyer's (employer's) market right now. You may be in a tight financial situation and can't afford a lengthy job search. There may be family and friends who pressure you not to look for a new job but rather to stay in your safe, dead-end one because it pays the bills. Or, you may be feeling distress for other reasons. Perhaps you have been out of the job market for a while and are scared about how you'll start up, much less make it all the way through a job search. Maybe you have always been recruited and pursued by employers. You haven't had to work hard to land a job in the past, but that situation has changed this time around. Perhaps you've just been through a bad time in your life and don't have a lot of energy or confidence to be doing a job search now. You wonder how you'll get motivated.

● FACING THE CHALLENGE

Whatever your reasons, doing a job search can be a real challenge. The biggest hurdle is usually the first step. It does become easier after that—I promise. The inertia—the strong force not to do anything, not to make a move, not to try a change or take a chance—can be paralyzing. This chapter offers hope, help, and practical steps you can take to get started on and conduct a successful job search.

Assess Yourself

Some of us go through life never taking the time to clarify for ourselves what we want in our work or career. Knowing yourself—your values, priorities, preferences, interests, and strengths—is the all-important foundation for a job search or a career change. As the saying goes, "It's difficult to get where you are going if you don't know where it is you want to go."

You'll need to start by asking yourself some tough questions and doing some soul searching. Set aside a few hours to think about the following:

- What do I value in my work, a job, my career?
- What are my short-term (within the next few years) and longer-term (five years out) priorities?
- What are my strong interests and loves? How can I incorporate these into my work?
- If I could be in any industry, organization, and job, what would I prefer?
- What are my strengths?
- Which of my strengths would I like to use in my next job or role?
- What provides meaning and purpose in my life?

- If I were writing a headline for a newspaper article about what my life vision is, what would that be?
- How does my work or career fit into the context of my total life vision?

Check out some additional resources for your self-assessment. Self-assessment indicators or inventories such as the MBTI (Myers-Briggs Type Indicator) and the BCII (Business Careers and Interests Inventory) can help you clarify your preferences and interests. They are often offered through your school's career center or alumni career services, private career coaches, community college career development courses, your company's Human Resources group, some career-related Web sites, and public career centers. Do a Google or Yahoo! key word search for the MBTI or BCII to see how you can take them.

Also, check out the Web sites at the end of this chapter or review my book, coauthored with Dr. Karen O. Dowd, *The Ultimate Guide to Getting the Career You Want and What to Do Once You Have It* (McGraw-Hill, 2003), which includes numerous self-assessment exercises.

Operating in Full Discovery Mode

Research and explore broadly. After you have completed your self-assessment, research and explore industries, companies, and jobs broadly. Learn about a wide spectrum of industries that interest you, organizations that you'd like working in, and kinds of jobs that you would enjoy and excel in. Allow your mind to wander, to dream, and to generate as many options as possible. Gain a sense for the range of possibilities.

Find out about as many industries, companies, and jobs as you can handle within the time you have set aside for your research. Include research on the long shots—those opportunities that may be more difficult to attain. You can make decisions and focus in later.

Keep your eyes wide open. Tap into the variety of resources for conducting your research: Web sites, your personal network, your alumni association, informational interviews with people in the industries, companies or jobs of interest, business periodicals, professional associations, and journals. Keep your eyes and ears open for what's available to you.

Be voracious. Use your time wisely but be insatiable in your appetite to find out what's of interest and is a fit for you. Unearth the possibilities—you owe it to yourself. For example, choose to use five to ten of the best job- and career-related Web sites. Call on the most promising people in your circle of friends and colleagues for job leads and referrals. Conduct informational interviews, during which you are fully prepared to get the most from the time spent. Read the top industry or professional periodicals for each of the industries you are exploring.

What to Look for in Your Research

Think about these dimensions for researching industries:

- What product(s) or service(s) does this industry actually offer?
- Who are the major players and the up-and-comers?
- What are the critical success factors for a company in the industry?
- What is the industry's reputation overall? What, if any, are the issues and concerns to watch out for?
- What is the outlook and hiring potential for this industry? Is it in hyper-growth mode, strong growth mode, decline, or close to extinction?
- What kinds of jobs does this industry have that could use what I have to offer?
- What type of talent does the industry attract, hire, and need?
- What is the ideal profile for someone to be a strong candidate for working in the industry?
- What are the specific three to five top strengths or kinds of experiences someone in this industry would need?

Use these as guidelines for researching companies and organizations:

- What differentiates this company from others in the industry?
- What are this company's culture, values, and priorities?
- What are its biggest challenges?
- How do I think it will fare?
- Who are its leaders (CEO, CFO, and COO and executive team)?

- What are their backgrounds and style?
- What do they seem to stand for?
- How does this company seem to treat its employees?
- What is the company's reputation?
- What do the media, customers, or others say about the company?
- What would it really be like to work there?

Consider these dimensions when researching jobs, fields, and professions:

- What do you actually do in this kind of job?
- What kind of colleagues does this kind of job/field/profession attract?
- How does someone today break into this industry or profession?
- What are the have-to-have skills, experience, and strengths needed to do the job successfully?
- What are the nice-to-haves—what is not required but preferred in candidates?
- How long do people typically stay in this kind of job?
- What are the possible next few moves?
- Longer term, what would a career path look like?
- Why do people leave this kind of job, field, or profession?
- Where do they typically go?

Networking Is Critical to a Job Search

Network smart. The new style of networking is about building a diverse circle of friends and contacts. Beginning with a few friends or contacts, you branch out from there, developing new relationships over time. The effective style of networking now is about a healthy, reciprocal give and take. You may ask for help from those in your network right now. In the future, people in your network may ask for your assistance or you may help each other's friends and family.

Contact your circle of friends and colleagues and ask for the specific help that you need. Networking is a great way to research industries, companies, and jobs or fields. It can also bring you actual job leads. That's because the people you'll be contacting are working themselves and therefore have employers or clients. They will also have their own circle of friends and colleagues to whom they may refer you. Overall, your network will be price-less as a valuable font of information and referrals. What these people share and how they help you will save you hours of other kinds of research or cold calling (contacting people you do not know).

Most people, although very busy, are willing to help. They like sharing their knowledge and advice. Make it easy for them to do so. And respect their time and limits. Start with your circle of friends and colleagues, and branch out from there. Take a look at Figure 1-1 in the section on marketing yourself for ideas on diversifying and expanding your network. Be clear about what you ask your network of contacts for. It could be:

- Information on their industry and the companies that are doing well
- Advice on how you can improve your chances and make your back-ground more competitive
- Ideas on getting your foot in the doors of their specific companies
- Leads for job openings or people who are hiring
- Referrals for your informational interviews

Network on the go. If you are like many people, you won't have a strong, effective network already in place. Perhaps you've been too busy to put the effort into it, found the concept of networking quid pro quo distasteful, or simply have not known how to build a network. You may have to develop your network on-the-go. Rich sources for your networking are:

- Your former and current colleagues
- Career services professionals from your high school, university, or graduate school
- Former and current teachers or professors and classmates
- People you have volunteered with
- Casual acquaintances from your social and outside-of-work activities such as your gym, sports team, religious group, the dog park, weight loss challenge group, reading club, film society, or neighborhood

- Parents of your children's friends
- Friends, family, and significant others of your siblings or parents

Tap your school resources. Get connected with your alumni association chapter in your city. Find out what events are being planned and get involved. You can easily and quickly meet people who share a sense of community and camaraderie. Volunteer to handle registration at an event so that you can meet people as they arrive. Help put together a networking program or job- or career-related committee. Also contact your school's alumni relations group. Ask what career services are offered to alumni. Many schools offer, for example, career advice by telephone or run career management workshops on self-assessment, changing industries, or résumé writing. They may host events to bring together both people looking for jobs and those who are hiring. Your alumni association or local chapter may also offer panel discussions from career experts or executives who do a lot of hiring. It will also most likely offer specialized resources for alumni careers such as handouts, job search survival kits, or access to job listings or an alumni database or directory.

Deciding Where to Focus

From your research and networking, you will have generated many options for yourself. Now it's time to zero in and determine where you'll focus your efforts. Which industries, companies, and kinds of jobs will you target? Make a list of what intrigues you most and what you want to pursue further. Which few industries are you interested in that are also a good fit for your values, interests, and preferences? Which are realistic to pursue? If you have a 50:50 chance, many would say those are strong odds in your favor. Make sure to include those you have a good shot at but also some that are a long shot.

Make your short list. Decide on the two or three industries and 10 to 20 organizations you'll try for. Figure out what kinds of jobs you will target, realizing that your strengths and experiences are often applicable to more than one kind of job. For example, you may have been a strategy consultant but have strengths and experience relevant for a strategic planning, marketing, or operations role. You may have been a banker but your skills, abilities, and knowledge are versatile enough to go for jobs as a venture capitalist, entrepreneur, or mutual fund manager.

Know who is hiring and when. Determine the general timing of your job search based on when your top-choice industries or companies tend to recruit. Some recruit heavily after the New Year. Others may hire year-round but primarily during a peak time once a quarter. Most companies recruit as the openings come up.

Understand how long it will take. If you're in school, expect to dedicate as much time to your job search as you would to an entire academic course. Mid-career to executive job seekers should expect to spend one to two months searching for every $10,000 of your targeted salary. For example, a job paying $100,000 could take 10 to 20 months to find. A job paying $50,000 could take five to ten months.

Marketing Yourself

Take a look at the Marketing 5 P's (Figure 1-1). Think about yourself as a product, a brand, or your own company: You, Inc. You will need to market yourself to potential customers-employers. To plan your marketing strategy, think of yourself in terms of the classic marketing 5 P's:

1. *Product:* What do you have to offer? What key strengths, skills, abilities, and attributes can you offer your potential employers? How will you convey these on your resume and in person?

2. *Price:* What is your value in the marketplace? What are you worth? Are you a premium product—something elite and in limited supply—or will you need to sell at a discount to get your foot in the door of your targeted industry?

3. *Promotion:* What core messages will you use about yourself and what you have to offer in your résumé, cover letter, interviews, and interactions? How can you best appeal to the employers you are targeting?

Figure 1-1. The Marketing 5 P's and the Branding of YOU

Key Considerations for Each P and Your Self-Marketing

Product
- Your benefits and attributes
- What you have to offer
- Your strengths

Price
- Your value in the market
- What you value in total compensation

Place/Distribution
- How you distribute your talents to the market
- Use of a multichannel approach

YOU

Positioning
- Your points of difference
- Value proposition relative to your competitors

Promotion
- How you make your talents known or compelling
- Not PR: communicating ideas on your strengths

---

4. *Place/Distribution:* How will you distribute yourself on the market? Consider using multiple means of delivering yourself to potential employers. This could include attending on-campus recruiting events if you are a student, applying to job ads, participating in career fairs, searching company Web sites, working with executive recruiters, and being referred by your network.

5. *Positioning:* What differentiates you from other candidates vying for the job? What is unique about you that is also relevant to the industry, company, and job?

Create stand-out résumés and cover letters. Résumés, cover letters, effective networking, and skillful interviewing are your most powerful self-marketing tools. They deserve more in-depth discussion by themselves. Chapter 3 discusses developing a winning résumé, handling common résumé problems, and writing cover letters that get you noticed. For more advice on networking, including specific how-to's on informational interviewing, refer to Chapter 17, "Making a Major Career Change."

Developing Your Action Plan

What actions do you need to take? What is the timing you will give yourself for accomplishing each or what is the deadline you are setting for yourself? In general, the top job-search to-do's are:

- Engage in as much self-assessment as you need to for understanding what you want, what you value, and your goals and objectives for your job search and next career move.
- Research and explore broadly which industries, organizations, and kinds of jobs you are interested in.
- Evaluate your options, your strengths, and your best fits; make decisions on what you'll pursue.
- Identify and use your network for your research as well as for job leads and referrals.
- Generate and follow up on job leads from a variety of sources that give you the most impact for the time invested—that net the most viable job opportunities for the time and effort you expend.
- Develop a winning résumé and stand-out cover letters. Send them out with focus and intent. Follow up with telephone calls or e-mails.
- Prepare and practice your interviewing skills.
- Prepare your compensation negotiation strategy and job offer evaluation criteria when you make it to the second round or in the more advanced interviewing stages. Decide how you will choose which offer to accept if you have multiple job offers.
- Monitor how you are doing. Ask for others' feedback or review yourself. Keep track of what you are doing, how you are doing, and where you can improve.
- Keep your enthusiasm and your momentum up. Blend into your job search people, activities, and rejuvenation breaks that fuel your inspiration, creativity, energy, and determination.

Implement, monitor, evaluate, motivate. Monitor how you are doing compared to your job-search action plan. As you move forward on your action plan, try to get feedback whenever possible to improve your performance. Ask for feedback from anyone who can provide constructive input on how you can be better: those who reviewed your résumé or rehearsed with you for interviewing; those with whom you did information interviews; and recruiters who interviewed you for a job. If you don't receive a lot of feedback, critique yourself. Evaluate yourself on the following:

- What is and isn't working?
- Where can I improve?
- What help or advice do I need?
- Where can I go for further help, resources, and expertise?
- How can I stay motivated to keep up my momentum?
- Are there gaps in my performance that need filling in?

These gaps could be, for example, knowledge shortcomings such as not using the industry terminology or not knowing how the industry really works. There could also be a gap in job-search skills such as how to interview or close the "deal" and get the offer.

● Tools and Resources

Be selective about which Web sites you use for your job search. Choose sites with large databases and good search features so you can pinpoint what you want quickly and net the best return on your investment of time. Also make sure to visit individual company Web sites. These are great for company-specific information. They will also give you a sense of the organization's culture, what they value, and their hiring outlook. On the company Web sites, look for overviews of products or services, biographies of the executives, profiles of representative career paths, job opportunities and how to apply for them, financial statements, media mentions and press clippings, and so on.

Overall Career Management
- Career Builder—*www.careerbuilder.com.* Career advice, articles, job postings from more than 35 localized news sites, such as Chicago tribune.com and BayArea.com. National and local job market opportunities.

- Career Inspirations—*www.career-inspirations.com*. Advice, articles, frameworks, and other valuable resources and information on job searches, career changes, career management for a lifetime, and recruiting strategies.
- Career Voyager—*www.careervoyager.com*. Offers advice, a collection of job sites, research resources, job-hunting news, interview questions, and information on job fairs, graduate schools, and professional associations.
- *Fast Company Magazine—www.fastcompany.com/*. An extensive online career center loaded with job search and career information. Check out the "company of friends," a collection of 150+ groups and thousands of members for networking, online discussions, and sharing advice.
- *New York Times—www.nytimes.com/jobs*. Great guide to how to use technology in job hunting; pointers to relevant Web resources such as online résumé preparation, work alternatives, networking in cyberspace, and so on. Job ads and collection of columns on careers.
- Quintessential Careers—*www.quintcareers.com*. Step-by-step process for the job search.
- Wet Feet Press—*www.wetfeet.com*. Numerous industry and company profiles, career advice and articles, and expert guides on topics such as compensation negotiation.
- *What Color Is Your Parachute/Job Hunters' Bible—www.jobhunters bible.com*. Information and steps for job hunters and career changers.

Job Listings and Employment Opportunities
- Headhunter.net—*www.headhunter.net/*. Permits posting your résumé online, receiving information about jobs by e-mail, searching for jobs by interests, and participating in virtual (online) career fairs.
- Jobs in the Money—*www.jobsinthemoney.com*. A job site dedicated to finance professionals interested in investment and commercial banks, Big 5 accounting firms, Fortune 500 companies, and technology companies, etc.
- JobStar—*http://jobsmart.org*. A site including information on the hidden job market, salary data, and *Wall Street Journal* stories on job

hunting and career management. Searchable database of more than 30,000 middle- and senior-level positions, updated daily. Career centers and libraries for California and beyond. Personal electronic librarian to answer your questions.

- Leaders Online—*http://leadersonline.com*. Exclusive management and senior-level career opportunities. In partnership with *Business Week Online*, it offers access to top employers, executive search firms, and venture capital companies.

- Monster.com—*www.monster.com*. Touts more than 1 million job postings. Can be used to research companies, search job listings, and find out your market value through a "personal salary report." Includes a global network of experts and resources. There is also information on and help with self-employment or contract/temporary work.

- *The Riley Guide—www.rileyguide.com*. A comprehensive listing of employment opportunities and job resources. Provides a directory of employment and career information sources and services on the Internet for job searching outside the United States. Links to resources and online job banks for Asia/Pacific Rim, Canada, Europe, Latin America, etc.

Also review the Top Ten list of resources in Chapter 16, "Surviving a Layoff."

Executive Recruiters

- FutureStep—*www.futurestep.com/*. Executive search service for management professionals from Korn/Ferry International and the *Wall Street Journal*. Offers access to exclusive opportunities with companies worldwide. Fosters long-term career management relationship, including an assessment tool and feedback on best fits for industries and companies. Members can send résumés to companies.

- Heidrick & Struggles—*www.heidrick.com*. Worldwide executive search firm specializing in chief executive, board of directors, and senior-level management assignments.

- Korn/Ferry International—*www.kornferry.com.* Globally recognized top search firm specializing in chief executive and senior management openings.
- Russell Reynolds—*www.russellreynolds.com.* Top-tier international search firm specializing in executive and senior management openings.
- Spencer Stuart Career Network—*www.spencerstuart.com.* Leading international search firm specializing in executive and senior management opportunities.

Sources for Researching Companies

- Bureau of Labor Statistics—*www.bls.gov.* An agency within the U.S. Department of Labor.
- *Business Week* Online—*www.businessweek.com.* Use the company research, compare salaries and living costs tools, and sign up for the career-related newsletters. Subscription fee.
- Hoovers Online—*www.hoovers.com.* Top research tool. Do an advanced search by area code and industry. Comprehensive company, industry, and market intelligence.

Company Lists and Profiles

- *Business Week*'s "The 100 Best Growth Companies"—*http://www .businessweek.com.* Excellent listing and background information on the top 100 growth companies and related articles/links.
- Corporate Financials Online—*www.cfonews.com.* Fast, direct links to news from publicly traded companies.
- Edgar Online—*www.sec.gov/edgarhp.htm.* A company database from the SEC.
- The Fortune Global 500—*http://www.fortune.com/fortune/fortune500.* View the companies, their rank, revenues, and company snapshots.
- *Fortune Magazine*'s Most Admired Companies—*www.fortune.com/ fortune/mostadmired.* Check out *Fortune*'s list of America's Most Admired Companies. This includes 592 + reputational scores, industry rankings, and related articles.
- The *Inc.* 500—*www.inc.com/inc500.* A list of America's fastest growing private companies.

- SiliconValley.com—*http://www.siliconvalley.com/mld/siliconvalley.* Job opportunities, business articles, and useful information about Silicon Valley companies and people.
- Wall Street Research Net—*www.wsrn.com.* Over 250,000 links for research on actively traded companies.
- Wetfeet.com—*www.wetfeet.com.* An overall stellar site with insider guides describing what it is like to work in different industries, companies, and fields (e.g., investment banking, management consulting, brand management, healthcare). You can also sign up for newsletters and benefit from informative articles on a broad range of job search, career change, and career management topics.

Aligning Your Values with Your Career Choices

HAVE YOU QUIT A JOB because it was not a fit with your values? For instance, you disagreed with an unethical boss, found the culture too competitive or combative, or didn't flourish under the management style? Have you changed employers a few times because you think you know what you're getting into when you accept the job but realize after being in the company for a while that it is not what you expected? Has your company recently merged with or been acquired by another company? Have you patiently waited to see what the newly formed organization would be like and concluded that with the new CEO and executives in power, the company values and culture have changed so much that they are not what you want? Are you seriously considering leaving the company because of a new manager or senior managers whose styles, ethics, and values are incongruent with yours?

● DEFINING THE CHALLENGE

The Enron debacle and other corporate wrongdoings exposed in the media the past few years have made all of us more aware of the importance of knowing who you work with and who you work for. It's true that the good, the bad, or the ugly usually starts at the top and trickles down.

Understanding your values, and making sure that the job and career choices you make are based on them, is a real challenge for many people. There are good reasons for this dilemma. First off, you simply may need a job, and this situation forces you to take whatever position comes along, without regard to the corporate culture. In many other cases, the job or company seems glamorous or cool, and you are lured by that. You don't take or have the time to do your due diligence—your research on the company's values—before you accept an offer. Perhaps you figure every job and every company have their negatives, and you are willing to overlook a few red flags because there are so many other positives you are drawn to.

Maybe it's even more complex than any of these reasons. You are not sure of your own values and what you stand for. You really don't know what's important to you in an employer. You just know what it is that you *don't want* or what turns you off about certain situations. You need to translate these feelings into what you *do want*.

● FACING THE CHALLENGE

We may not be able to articulate it cogently, but each of us has a value system—what we hold dear, stand for, and use as an internal compass for guiding our actions and behavior. In my work advising executives, managers, and students, I have found that those who tend to be happiest, most fulfilled, and satisfied in their work and careers are in work situations—in jobs, in organizations, or working with clients—that are in alignment with their own values.

You'll find it much easier to achieve this alignment during your job search rather than after you've taken a job. This chapter guides you on how to conduct your research, evaluate the dimensions of your values vis-à-vis a potential employer's values, and ask the tough questions to assess the situation.

Look for Alignment

Taking the time to ask the tough questions and to evaluate the companies you are considering—before you join them—is key to making informed, values-based decisions in your job search.

Make it a search and review mission. Find out as much as you can about the organization, the CEO and executive team, your potential manager, and the general value system that prevails in the company. It is imperative to learn as much as you can about a potential employer as early as possible.

Be clear on your own values. Start with a strong foundation of knowing what is important to you. Is it money, power, fame, the big corner office, being on the "A" list of "in" people? Is it doing work that you love, providing financially for your family, having time for family and outside interests, or knowing at the end of the day that you are making a difference to something bigger than yourself that you believe in? Be honest with yourself about what you truly value. Prioritize your values. Write them down so you have them to refer to when you are evaluating organizations and offers. Think about what each of those values means to you.

Make the translation. How will your values translate—manifest themselves—in a corporate culture, values system, and company leadership? How will those values look in actions, behaviors, attitudes, policies, processes, or management styles? What do you value in an employer? For example, if money and power are important to you, perhaps you would like to work in an organization that values competition or a star system, or that tolerates healthy egos. On the other hand, if doing what you love or having a lot of family time are what you value, maybe you should choose an employer where career-broadening moves and being allowed to grow into a job are supported. With such an employer, there probably would also be policies and practices that encourage family leave and reasonable or at least flexible work schedules.

Dial it up a notch. Beyond your own values and what you value in an employer, what about the executive team? What do you value in a CEO, the senior managers, and your own boss? Do these key leaders stand for what you believe in and will their actions respect others, treat employees fairly, involve healthy risks, and tolerate mistakes, too? Do they embody attitudes and behaviors that shout "win at all costs"? Will they want to be the first to market and engage in cutthroat competition? These are extreme examples, but they highlight the dramatic differences among what organizations value and how they act with their employees and customers.

Read between the lines. Take a look at the company's Web site, its annual report, and recruitment literature. Do a search on Google or Yahoo! for media stories on the company or its leaders. Does the company have a values statement, an aspirations statement, or a code of ethics? Is what is espoused in sync with the photos, the sound bites, and the company's track record? For example, does the company say it values diversity, but everyone in the photos or whom you see at the career fairs looks the same, even down to the way they dress? Does the company say it values its employees, but there are three class-action suits against it for unfair salary or promotional practices? Does the company say it values innovation, integrity, and growth, and, by way of proof, it has been named one of "The Most Admired Companies in America" in the last ten years?

Get the Facts

Ask insiders for the straight scoop. When you meet with people from the company, ask them what the company values. Press for examples. If Joe Smith tells you that the company values risk taking, but he can't give you examples of his or his colleagues' taking risks, then something is not right. If Jane Dawson tells you that the company is very collaborative and not hierarchical, but every interaction you have had is rigidly chain-of-command, then there's a disconnect somewhere. Trust your gut instincts. Determine if the information you glean is a deal breaker for you, meaning that you would walk away from an offer with that company.

Do your due diligence. Dig deep and be tenacious in finding out what the CEO and executive team stand for. Often they may embody different values from those the workforce holds. They may be out of touch or operating on a different playing field. The harsh reality, however, is that the CEO is the person steering the ship. He or she and the executive team are huge influences on the performance of the company, as well as on the day-to-day environment and culture—the overall value system—you would be working in.

Mine the data. You may not be able to meet the CEO or all the executive team members, but unearth and take a close look at whatever information you can get. For example, try some of the following:

- Read the CEO and executive team's bios. You can learn much more than you may first think from such material. What motivated them to be in the organization or industry? What are their backgrounds and do they show any biases? What can you make of the kind of people they are? What do they seem to value—being featured in the media, acquiring wealth, spending time with their families, developing their employees, being innovative, or creating positive change?
- Review speeches they have made that may be on the company's Web site or excerpted in press clippings. True, these may be sound bites, but if they are repeated often enough, they must mean something to someone.
- Search on Google and Yahoo! for background information or articles about the CEO and executive team members. Typing in their first and last names in quotation marks probably will be all that's necessary to find the related links.
- Ask people within the company what they think about the CEO and top management. Of course, this would not be the first question out of your mouth. You would want to wait until you are pretty far along in the recruiting process and have established a relationship with those you are interviewing or talking with.
- Utilize the opportunity to hear the CEO or an executive team member speak, whether at an event or if he or she interviews you. Be well prepared to ask the individual questions and to evaluate what he or she stands for and values.

Ask the tough questions. Ask questions and find out information as you are meeting with and interviewing people in the organization. Essentially, interview the company and your interviewers. Make it a priority to ask the tough questions now so that you can make informed choices later about whether this is a viable organization that fits your values. Would you resonate in this environment and do well with this company? Take a look in the next section for a list of 30 questions to think about, ask, or research the answers to.

● TOOLS AND RESOURCES

Choose a few of these questions and pepper them throughout your research on the company, including during the interviewing process.

Values-Based Questions for Potential Employers

- What are the company's vision, values, and purpose?
- What is its mission?
- How does the company treat its employees in terms of career development, the hiring process, firing or laying off, compensation and benefits, raises and promotions?
- What is the company view on family commitments?
- What programs and policies are there that support employees with families?
- How does the organization value people of color? Give an example.
- How does the organization value women? Give examples.
- Can someone be a terrible manager and still keep his or her job?
- What happens to people who deliver bad news or problems to management?
- What happens when someone makes a big mistake or fails?
- What is considered success here?
- How does success get recognized?
- How are raises decided?
- How are promotions decided?
- How is performance evaluated? For example, is it all from the manager's point of view or does it incorporate 360 degree feedback (input from the person's manager, peers, and any direct reports)?
- How do people communicate with each other?
- How is conflict or disagreement handled?
- Describe the work environment here—what is it really like to work here?
- How do people feel about the organization?
- What's a typical work schedule for someone in this job? Do people take vacations or wind up losing them because they have the maximum amount "banked"?
- Do people work more collaboratively or individually?
- To what extent do people interact socially after work?
- How easy is it to ask for help or resources?
- How are resources like budget dollars or headcount allocated?

- How are differences of opinion handled?
- How does the CEO interact with employees?
- How about the other executives?
- What's the level of competition here?
- What are the office politics like?
- Why do people leave here? For example, why have the last three people you've known left the company?

Creating a Strong Résumé

HAVE YOU BEEN sending out a gazillion résumés and cover letters but they don't seem to be working? Are they not generating any interest or follow-up interviews? Do you feel insecure about what your résumé says about you or if it will stand up to the other candidates' résumés? Is your résumé out-dated? Has it not seen the light of day for a long while? Perhaps it's in a time warp, circa the 1980s. Are you about to embark on a job search, make a major career change, or want to be considered for a prime board of directors position and need a résumé that will convey the best of who you are and help you snag the role? How about those gaps in your résumé? Are you trying to make a comeback from a career break and need a fresh, well-positioned résumé to help you reenter the world of work? Maybe you are going for a career-broadening move in a completely different area in your company and need a résumé that will persuade the hiring manager that you do have the skills, abilities, knowledge, and potential to perform in the new job, although you don't have the formal experience. If any of this sounds like your situation, this chapter can help.

● DEFINING THE CHALLENGE

An effective résumé is a critical part of your self-marketing plan. It is a strategic communication that highlights your skills, abilities, and knowledge as they relate to the job or career change you are seeking. It is a focused sketch of your educational, professional, and personal background tailored to the position you are pursuing. Your résumé should be straightforward, logical, easy to read, and intriguing. The objective is to develop a winning, general résumé as a base. You can then use your base résumé to tweak and to customize, if you want to, for each different industry, company, or kind of job you are targeting.

A résumé can truly open or slam shut employers' doors. While your résumé won't actually get you the job, it will either help you get an interview or not. If your résumé doesn't grab the reviewer's attention within the first 10 to 15 seconds, it's likely that it will go in the "no" pile, given the overabundance of candidates and résumés these days. The problem with a résumé, bottom line, is when it is ineffective, or not serving to get you noticed by the person reviewing it.

Résumés can be a problem and can actually work against you if they are outdated or if they don't tell a cohesive, compelling story about your background and what your capabilities are. Résumés that are too wordy, disorganized, boring, suffer from unexplainable gaps in employment, or shout "job hopper," are red flags for employers. They'll be put in the reject pile without further consideration, leaving you out of the competition for the job.

● FACING THE CHALLENGE

This chapter gives you some fresh ideas on how to make your résumé stand out from the crowd. It will help you put your best foot forward. It will help you get noticed. How to handle common résumé problems is also discussed. These issues include:

- When to use a functional or a skills-based résumé
- What's best when you are changing careers
- How to quantify and calibrate your work experience
- How to deal with gaps in employment
- What to do if you have no degree or one from an unknown school
- What to do if you have worked for companies that are unknown

Résumé Types

There are essentially two kinds of résumés. *Reverse chronological* is the most widely used in business and other fields. Your education and work experience (organization names and titles) are listed most current first, sequenced through to the least current last. A second common type of résumé is a *functional* or *skills-based* résumé. These can be extremely valuable to those making major career changes. In the work experience section of the functional résumé, the focus is on three or four major skill sets that you possess and that are highly relevant to the job you are going for. From your sum total of work experiences (paid, unpaid, or volunteer), you pull out accomplishments that support each skill set on your résumé.

For a functional or skills-based résumé, you can list in one section all the organizations for which you worked, date ranges (month/year to month/year or whole year to whole year) and job titles and locations. Following this, you then list the three or four skill set headings. Under each skill set heading, you include a few bullet points of PAR (Problem-Action-Result) statements or a paragraph on what you accomplished to show how you have that skill.

Developing a Successful Résumé

Think two-dimensionally. Consider your résumé in terms of both style and content. While the content of your résumé is obviously critical, you must set it up in a way that quickly draws the attention of the recruiter. A résumé filled with great work experience and accomplishments is worthless if nobody reads it.

Style

Make it easy to read. Style covers things like font style and size, formatting (if you use bullets or paragraphs), how you will show your dates (month/year is okay, but full years is best—e.g., 2001–present), locations, and section headers. The objectives of style are to make your résumé easy to read and comprehend quickly because someone who is not familiar with your background will be reading it.

Make it look inviting. You want your résumé to look professional, neat, and uncluttered. You want your chosen information to flow in an easy-to-follow way. Pay attention to the details. Remember that anything you put in bold type, or italicize, or put in all caps, will stand out to the reader, so use these eye-catchers sparingly. Watch out for what I call clutter to the eyes. This includes underlines, parentheses, and quotation marks. Stay away from these. Try to make every word count. Don't be afraid of white space; your résumé will be easier to read and cleaner-looking if it is not filled to the edges with words.

Aim for one page. Include the three or four common sections mentioned below in your résumé and try to keep it to one page. If you have extensive experience—several jobs or titles and/or changing industries and/or are going for a highly technical job—then you may need to use a two-pager. If you do, make sure to put your initial and last name on the bottom right-hand side of each page—for example, "G. Alberts, 1 of 2" on the first page, then "G. Alberts, 2 of 2" of the second page.

Core Content

Include three or four sections in your résumé. The common sections are discussed here along with what each one should include.

- *Identification Information (name, how to contact you).* An up-to-date résumé will also include your cell phone number and your e-mail address.
- *Work Experience.* Present your PAR statements in bullet format or paragraphs. PAR statements are discussed in the next section, Breaking Down Your Work Experience.
- *Education.* This would include actual earned degrees or relevant coursework. A few of your most impressive honors, affiliations, or activities would be okay here, too. An interesting, attention-grabbing thesis, field study, or research project would be great to mention, especially if your experience is slim in the other areas.
- *Additional Information or Other.* If you feel it is needed, use this section to round you out, make yourself a stronger candidate for the job, or make yourself more interesting. This section may be used to underscore technical knowledge or skills, such as Oracle systems knowledge or HTML or C++ programming, or certification in a

course or training that would be useful for the new job—for example, completion of a conflict-resolution training program or being a graduate of the Wharton Executive Education Course on Financial Management. Other items typically included are language capabilities if relevant (e.g., fluent in Spanish) and hobbies or interests that round you out as a person, make you a stronger candidate, or simply make you seem more interesting. Remember: This section is the last impression you leave, so end with a vivid picture.

Breaking Down Your Work Experience

The critical part of your content section is work experience. What you choose to say and how you say it can make the difference in developing a winning or a losing résumé.

Stress your accomplishments. Build your work experience section on PAR statements. I like to call these accomplishment statements. Call out what in your background is relevant to the new job and the organization you are trying to join. If you are changing careers, focus on transferable skills, experience, and knowledge.

A PAR statement is composed of three parts:

1. The Problem—or issue that you solved; a need or challenge that you met; a major undertaking you made.
2. The Action—what you did; the action(s) you took.
3. The Result—what the benefit or outcome was for the organization. Try to quantify or calibrate the result.

Essentially, you state a problem that you took on. You convey what action you took. You describe the result. Examples of phrases that can be used in accomplishment statements include:

- "Improved quality or response time"
- "Increased profits with . . ."
- "Reduced costs"
- "Grew the business"

- "Strengthened morale"
- "Enhanced productivity"
- "Lowered turnover"
- "Designed a new program"
- "Created a new process to improve, reduce, or change . . ."
- "Decreased failures, shrinkage, overtime, or downtime"

No fifth wheel. Remember that you will want to cite only the most compelling achievements and accomplishments. If it's a fifth wheel, of no use, leave it off your résumé. Use the criteria below when determining which specific work experiences you will use for your PAR statements:

- Your contribution produced something important to your organization, the employees, or your clients/stakeholders.
- You reached results with fewer resources, under budget, before the deadline.
- You made something easier, simpler, better, or faster.
- You achieved something for the first time or performed remarkably given the circumstances.
- You or others were proud of what you did; it made a difference.

Quantify and calibrate. For work experience, quantify as best you can. Give numbers, results, percentages, or other specifics whenever you are able to. To calibrate, provide some relativity to the bigger picture or some context so the person reviewing your résumé gains a sense of just how big, how great, how difficult, how important, how valuable, or how impressive—that is, how much of a difference your contribution made in the whole scheme of things.

Quantifying Examples
- "Contributed to team that designed and tested $5 million inventory system. Result led to Fortune 100 client saving $25 million annually."
- "Created and ran training course on customer service, which resulted in 54% higher ratings from customer survey."

- "Managed eight-person team to reengineer the staff scheduling process for a major airline client, resulting in 15% reduction in cost."

Calibrating Examples
- "Invited to stay on as third-year investment banking analyst. Consistently ranked among top 5% of peer group."
- "Youngest in-resident choreographer in repertory's 50-year history."

What to Leave Out

Avoid unnecessary details. Don't include in your résumé salary history or requirements, references, or reasons for termination. These are for later, to be discussed in your interviews, when you are being seriously considered for the job.

Don't brag or be trite. There is a fine line between marketing yourself and your abilities to the fullest and overdoing it. For the most part, do not make exaggerated or overzealous statements. Also avoid overused phrases such as "the ultimate team player," "driven to succeed," or "a quick study."

Fine-Tuning Your Résumé

Be choosey. Include in your résumé only what you would want to be asked about. Remember that your résumé is not a laundry list of everything you have ever done. Its main purpose is to pull out the highlights and convey them in a compelling and interesting way. Keep in mind that everything on your résumé is fair game for the interviewer to probe into. Be able to speak knowledgeably and in depth about anything on your résumé.

Check it out. Don't make your poor grammar, spelling, or syntax be what the interviewers or employers focus on in your résumé. Let it be your great work experience and education, or other strengths that they notice. Errors in grammar, spelling, syntax, or even inconsistent or sloppy formatting indicate that you are careless, rushed, or didn't take your résumé seriously. Meticulously check and double-check for grammar and spelling errors.

Check your sentence structure. Let someone with a fresh pair of eyes and good attention to detail read your résumé and provide feedback.

How to Handle Common Résumé Problems

There are a few common problems that you can overcome effectively. Each problem is discussed with a few example fixes/suggestions.

Gaps in your employment. I always vote for complete honesty, but you don't have to let a gap be a negative. If possible, note the gap but give a short explanation for it. Examples are:

- "Took 6 months off to care for terminally ill mother."
- "Took one year off to train and try out for professional women's volleyball."

No degree. If you have no degree but have equivalent work experience, really emphasize your work experience section, showing that you possess the knowledge and skills required for the job. List in the "additional info" section any training courses you have taken or self-initiated studies that are relevant to the job. Examples are:

- "Studied operations and accounting through own initiative."
- "Participated in marketing seminars."
- "Self-taught in finance through volunteer projects and various online courses."

An unknown school. Say something positive about the school to give some context if you can. Examples are:

ALAN PEARSON SCHOOL OF DESIGN—
"Leading school of fashion design in the West Coast region, known for planet-friendly packaging and apparel."

LEEWICK COLLEGE
"East Coast liberal arts college founded in 1956 with reputation for well-rounded graduates. Notable alumni include _____."

If there is nothing you can say about the school itself, then emphasize your activities by listing a few of the key ones, mention your academic standing if you were in the top 10 percent of your class, or describe your thesis or fieldwork if they are appropriate to making you a stronger candidate for a job.

An unknown company. Perhaps you are working for a terrific company that is known in some circles but may not be where you'll be targeting your job search. Add a brief description of the company after the organization's name; an example is:

MARKETOCRACY

"A visionary mutual fund management company that recruits the best stock pickers in the world by tracking the performance of over 70,000 virtual model portfolios. Recognized by *Business Week* as one of the best."

Developing a Functional Résumé

Functional résumés are more challenging to develop, and often they are not done well. Because they are also not the norm—the typical kind of résumé a recruiter would be seeing—it is imperative that you make this résumé above and beyond the ordinary; that is, it should be exceptional.

Here are some ideas to help you develop a functional résumé, plus an example excerpt of a functional résumé work experience section:

- List the organizations, titles, years in the job, and locations (cities and states or countries) for the work experience you are highlighting. They should be sequenced, either most current to least current or least current to most current.
- List either the organizations or the titles first, then the other one second, but make sure to be parallel—be consistent about the order. Choose to lead off with what's most impressive; sometimes that's title. Other times it is a well-known, respected company name.

Example of a Functional Résumé

In the following example, the skill headings are "Client Relationships," "Research and Analysis," "Communication," and "Teamwork and Leadership."

We derive the bullet points supporting each skill set from the sum total of this person's jobs and employers to develop compelling PAR statements for each skill set.

WORK EXPERIENCE

McKinsey and Co., *Business Analyst,* 1997–1999, Chicago, IL

Google, Inc., *Lead German Language Translator,* 1999–2002, Mountain View, CA

Golf Adventures, Inc., *Cofounder,* 2002–present, Monterey, CA
Golf pro services to high net worth individuals; provider of Outward Bound–type team building and leadership training for small to large companies using golf. Recently named one of the Bay Area's fastest growing small companies. [Note: we use a description of Golf Adventures since it is an unknown company.]

CLIENT RELATIONSHIPS

- Worked on three different engagement teams while consulting; interacted extensively with client management and employees.
- Proactively cultivated relationships and potential clients for golf business; received high marks with wide range of people, senior managers to administrators. Return business rate is 80% and more than half our new business is from word of mouth.

RESEARCH AND ANALYSIS

- Conducted competitive research on SUV manufacturers, assessed hybrid car market potential, and designed and analyzed client satisfaction surveys and focus groups for a top-three automobile manufacturer.

COMMUNICATION

- Rated as "excellent" communicator in all client surveys.
- Authored numerous reports, such as industry studies, research findings, and client focus group findings.

- Enjoy creative writing and hearing people's points of view; design and run own blog related to classical guitar music.
- Highly skilled in PowerPoint presentations and using visuals to tell stories or illuminate complex concepts.

TEAMWORK AND LEADERSHIP

- Served as co-captain for undergraduate recruiting at seven midwestern universities; mentored the new hires.
- Facilitated team-building exercises and simulations for groups of 5–50 in Golf Adventures, Inc.
- Worked with Europe-based counterparts to translate Google content for German market. Shared and received ideas for new content.

Writing Targeted, Timely, Relevant Cover Letters

A résumé is not a stand-alone document. To prove most effective, a résumé needs an intriguing cover letter to introduce it and set it up contextually. The best cover letters are focused, not reflective of a mass mailing. Cover letters must be targeted, timely, and relevant. Here are some fine points.

Make it personal. Address letters to a person and make each letter unique. Ideally this would be the decision maker or hiring manager, HR point person, or whomever you are asked to send your résumé to. It could also be someone you know within the organization (asking the person to refer your letter and résumé to the appropriate individual).

Keep it brief. Try for about ³/₄ page or a maximum of 1¹/₂ pages.

Be direct. Use simple and direct language. Maintain a balanced tone. Try for not too formal and not too casual. Your letter should sound like you are speaking to the person—like you are engaging the individual in a conversation.

Make it sound like you are already a fit. Focus on the needs, style, and culture of the organization. Try to identify through your research what the company wants, what it needs, and its culture. Write your letter as though you are already a great fit with the organizational style, values, and culture. Write as though they need to hire you!

Spare the details. Do not repeat details from your résumé. That would be redundant and a waste of valuable attention time. Craft a few compelling lead-in sentences for your letter that make the reader intrigued to read your résumé.

Don't come across as pretentious. At all costs, avoid arrogant statements, shameless name-dropping, or uninformed assertions.

Use adjectives sparingly. Do not use too many adjectives. Try to be concise, using the fewest number of words to say what you mean. Make every word count.

Go easy on jargon and buzzwords. Avoid jargon, pat phrases, and trite expressions such as "I am a self starter"; "You will not find anyone as enthusiastic or qualified as I am"; "I can help you meet your challenges. . . ."

Be real. Let your interest, enthusiasm, and what you have to offer shine through.

Read, reread, and review again your cover letter. Just as for your résumé, review your cover letter meticulously for typos, grammar, spelling mistakes, and the like. Find someone with a fresh pair of eyes to proofread both your letter and your résumé, as well as to give you feedback on the whole package. Review the following outline as a guide.

Cover Letter Outline

A cover letter typically is composed of four parts:

1. *An introduction.* Summarize who you are and the purpose of your letter. Name the person who referred you if applicable. Ask for an informational interview if that is what you want. If you are applying for a specific job, note which that is and how you learned of it.

2. *Interest highlights.* Offer an overview of what interests you about the company, its business, unique needs, or challenges, or why you are intrigued to make a move into the industry.

3. *Compelling examples.* Describe in brief, compellingly and succinctly, what you can offer. This could be relevant experience, particular strengths, or other skills, abilities, or knowledge that would be valuable to the organization. Make them interested in you! Get their attention on how you are a fit or would be an excellent candidate to consider.

4. *The close.* State your next steps. When you will follow up, how, and with whom.

Sample Cover Letters

1. REQUESTING AN INTERVIEW FOR A SPECIFIC JOB

I learned about your [*xyz*] job from Cameron Jones, who was your manager when you both worked together at [*abc*] company. Cameron and I are friends from our college days.

For the past eight years I have worked as a _____ [*title*] in a similar industry to yours, _____[*your current industry*]. The incredible experiences I have gained, projects to which I have enjoyed contributing, and people with whom I have worked, make me committed to taking the next step in my career.

With [*number*] years of experience in a variety of well-respected companies, I believe my strengths of _____, _____, and _____ make me an especially strong fit with MKT Company. I am very interested to discuss your [*xyz*] opportunity with you.

I will call your office early next week to ask about a time to meet. Thank you for your consideration.

2. REQUESTING AN INFORMATIONAL INTERVIEW

Matt Damone, who worked with you at Google, suggested I ask for your advice and insights. I am making a career shift out of high tech and am very interested in The GAP and the retail industry in general. You made the successful transition a while ago, and I would appreciate about 20 minutes of your time to learn from your experience.

I believe that with my current inventory management experience and previous years of merchandising experience, retail is a vibrant fit with my interests and background.

I can be flexible regarding your schedule and the best way for us to meet. I will call your office next week to arrange a time. If it's not possible to connect in person given your schedule, I could send you some questions by e-mail.

Many thanks.

● TOOLS AND RESOURCES

Favorite Résumé Action Verbs

Accomplished	Achieved	Adapted	Advised
Apprenticed with	Approved	Arranged	Assessed
Assisted	Authored	Backed up	Built
Collaborated	Conceived	Completed	Constructed
Consulted	Created	Cultivated	Decided
Delegated	Designed	Determined	Developed
Directed	Doubled	Edited	Engineered
Established	Evaluated	Experimented	Facilitated
Finessed	Formulated	Founded	Gained
Gathered	Generated	Grew	Guided
Handled	Headed	Helped	Imagined
Implemented	Improved	Initiated	Innovated
Instituted	Integrated	Invented	Justified
Led	Made	Managed	Mastered
Negotiated	Orchestrated	Ordered	Organized
Originated	Outpaced	Partnered with	Performed
Planned	Prepared	Problem solved	Produced
Project managed	Rebuilt	Recommended	Reduced

Reenergized	Reinvigorated	Regulated	Reorganized
Researched	Resolved	Retrenched	Reviewed
Revised	Scheduled	Self taught	Simplified
Sold	Solidified	Solved	Started Up
Strategized	Streamlined	Synthesized	Taught
Transformed	Translated	Tripled	Turned Around
Unified	Ushered in	Won	Worked with

Web Tools: Résumé and Cover Letter Help

- Career Lab—*www.careerlab.com/letters/default.htm.* Over 200 samples and examples of cover letters.
- JobStar: Résumé Banks—*http://jobstar.org/tools/resume/index.htm.* Résumé tips and examples including information on electronic résumé banks.
- JobStar: Cover Letters—*http://jobstar.org/tools/resume/cletters.htm.* Tools and samples for your cover letters.

Learning to Interview Well

ARE YOU NERVOUS before an interview, with a queasy stomach, sweaty palms, a pounding heart, or a dry mouth? Do you lack confidence in your interviewing skills or have you had some bad experiences in past interviews that make you insecure about your ability to perform? Do you suffer from foot-in-the-mouth syndrome or from brain dysfunction when you come face to face with the interviewer? Do you make it through the initial interviews but don't fare too well in the follow-up interviews when the pressure and intensive questions are turned up a notch? Perhaps you don't suffer from any of the above, but you do want to perform better in your interviewing. You want a competitive edge in your interviewing because you know that you are competing with extremely talented and well-prepared candidates for the same jobs. You want to be and to do your best.

Maybe you are not starting to interview for actual jobs just yet but have a few informational interviews lined up. Are you familiar with how to conduct them? Do you know what to do and not to do to make the interviewee and your time most productive?

● DEFINING THE CHALLENGE

Interviewing for most people does not come naturally. We are not born to interview. Interviewing is, however, a skill that can be developed. In fact, you can work on it so effectively that you actually ace your interviews. Acing the interviews means that you do so well in them that you feel great afterwards and know that you could not have done any better. As the golf legend Arnold Palmer once said, "The more I practice, the luckier I get." Interviewing, like other skills, takes focused effort and determined persever- ance. The more you practice, the luckier (and better) you will get.

● FACING THE CHALLENGE

The tips shared here are gleaned from 18 years of recruiting and interview- ing thousands of candidates for jobs ranging from CEO, to vice presidents, directors, managers, and individual contributors. Additional insights come from advising companies on how to recruit and from coaching those in job searches on interviewing skills.

Prelude to an Interview

Revisit your self-assessment work. Before you begin your interviewing, reflect on what you learned about yourself in your self-assessment exercise in Chapter 1. What are you looking for in a job, a career, and an employer? What's important to you? What are your priorities? Why are you interview- ing for this particular job? Revisit your values, interests, preferences—the kinds of roles and responsibilities that you want. Consider your top five criteria for choosing a company to join. Why are you excited about talking with the organization? What strengths do you have to offer? Reflecting on these dimensions will keep you focused in your interviews and keep you from wasting time (yours and the interviewer's).

Study your job search action plan, particularly the marketing 5 P's. See Chapter 1 and Figure 1-1 for a discussion of the 5 P's. What would you say about each product, place, promotion, price, and positioning? Articu- late to yourself what you have to offer: your skills, experience, education, talents, and strengths. What makes you unique? What are your points of difference? Understand how these make you a good fit for the opportunity the company is offering, so you can make the fact that you *are* a good fit clear to the interviewer.

Create a clear picture of what you have to offer. Formulate a picture of what you have to offer to the job and the organization for which you are interviewing. What can you do or offer that will make an impact on its business needs and challenges. What difference will you offer to make to this organization?

Formulate your message. What are the key themes or the important message you want to convey about yourself? If I were to read your résumé, what would I take away quickly about you? What is the underlying message you are sending in your résumé while you are telling the compelling but brief story of who you are, where you have been, what you have done, and what you are capable of doing in your next job, career, or organization.

Know your résumé inside and out. If you include something on your résumé, it's fair game to be asked about by the interviewer. If you say in your work experience that you developed a new inventory system or created a PR strategy to launch a new product, you could be asked how you did it, why you did it, what happened when you did it, what didn't work that you tried, and so on. If the accomplishment or fact is important enough to be on your résumé, then be prepared to discuss it in depth, whatever the questions.

Be honest. Even in the "Additional Information" section, if you say you enjoy wine tasting, then that should be true and you should be able to talk about wine. A candidate who is asked, for example, what his or her favorite wine is and who replies "white" is not going to score points or make a positive impression. His or her veracity would be questioned after an answer like that, as well as the good judgment of including this item on the résumé. Small things can make a big difference as to whether you are invited for further interviews.

As another example, if you say you are "fluent in French," then you may be expected to carry on the interview in that language with a native speaker on the spot. I have known many recruiters to test the candidate's language abilities right from the get-go, with no warning. If your language abilities are a strong suit for the job or company, note it, by all means. Just be clear about your level of skill in the language.

Be Ready for Anything

Anticipate. Anticipate the questions you think you will be asked. Make a list of them. As I've said, everything on your résumé is fair game. Other questions could derive from interactions or communications you have had with company representatives. Mentally note or jot down the key points you would emphasize in answering each question the interviewer could ask. Additionally, prepare how you would handle any illegal, unfair, or politically incorrect questions in a firm but graceful manner.

From researching the industry and company, and any interactions you have had so far, you should have a feel for what's important to and valued by the organization. For example, if a company is known for its ethics, you may be asked about an ethical dilemma you faced and how you handled it. If an industry or company is in hyper-growth mode, you may be asked about times you had to learn quickly, work in a fast-paced environment, and so on. If a company's culture is highly collaborative with lots of teamwork, you can bet that you will be asked something about working effectively in groups and handling conflict, or how your peers, direct reports, or boss would describe working with you.

Identify your weaknesses or question marks. Put yourself in the employer's shoes and think about what concerns or issues the employer would have about you and your qualifications for the job. What are the red flags or question marks about your background? Be ready to speak compellingly to dispel those. There are some common questions that employers across all industries tend to ask. A top 25 list is included at the end of this chapter.

Practice, but don't sound overrehearsed. Get practice on being interviewed to the point that you feel confident and comfortable in any situation. Start by taking your list of anticipated questions and listening to your answers out loud. Try mock interviews. Ask a friend or colleague, preferably in the industry or kind of job you are targeting, to ask you questions and simulate a real interview. The next time, videotape your mock interview so that you can see yourself and see how you can improve. Make sure to ask for honest, constructive feedback and suggestions for improving. Anything you want to build skill and competence in takes practice. Sports, making a speech or a toast, writing a report, or cooking a turkey dinner usually get better with practice. The more you interview, the better you will perform.

Prepare for when it's your turn to ask questions. Most interviewers will ask if you have questions at the end of an interview. If you don't have any, you may appear disinterested, unprepared, or as someone who does not take the initiative. Preparing questions for when it's your turn is an easy thing to do and can reap big rewards. Take 20 minutes to develop five questions that are good for *any* interview. Then take another 20 minutes before each interview to customize a few to make them more specific to the job or organization. A list of my favorite questions to ask recruiters or interviewers is included at the end of this chapter.

Interviewing Etiquette

Break the ice with aplomb. Be polite and connect with the interviewer. Offer a firm handshake and eye contact with a smile when you introduce yourself. Make a few minutes of small talk. Sample topics are:

- The weather
- Sports
- The technically advanced or "green" (environmentally conscious) corporate offices in which you are interviewing
- An award the company recently won
- An interesting story about the company's CEO that you recently read
- The new product that the company introduced and that you have tried
- A talk you recently heard from a company executive or someone from the company you had an interesting discussion with

Know your etiquette. As Forrest Gump might say, "Etiquette is what etiquette does." Your polite, gracious, and respectful actions and behavior in the interviews are fully in play with the interviewer. Etiquette is about treating the other person as you would wish to be treated, following the Golden Rule. Etiquette today means:

- Turning off your cell phone and pager
- Arriving on time and prepared for the interview
- Not wearing a ton of perfume or cologne since the person may have allergies
- Dressing appropriately for the interview; ideally, dress as if you already belong in the company at the level or the one above the job for which you are interviewing (take your clues from the company's annual reports, photos of employees and executives on the Web site, or managers you've seen representing the company at an event)
- Thanking the interviewer for his/her time and consideration
- Reiterating your genuine interest in and enthusiasm for the job and company

After the Interview

Ask for feedback. After you are interviewed, ask casually if the recruiter has feedback on how you can improve your interviewing skills. Tell her that you are always interested in learning how to be better. This can work to your advantage because it shows that you are open to learning and are secure enough to handle constructive feedback.

Make your interview matter. Follow up with a personalized thank-you letter within the next few days, no matter how busy you are. A personal handwritten note is a nice, classy touch. It's a welcome and gracious break from e-mail and voice mail, too. Sending a note by e-mail is also okay if the employer has a heavy e-mail culture.

Make your follow-up count. Use the follow-up to help the person remember you by recalling something you two "shared"—a funny story, side comment, or similar philosophy or experience. Reiterate your genuine interest in the organization and being able to contribute substantially. Include a reason or two why you would be so excited to work for the company. Affirm a few strengths or specific experience you have that would be valuable to the company.

Guide to Informational Interviewing

While you should be preparing for actual interviews during your job search, conducting a few informational interviews before any real ones is helpful. Informational interviews are helpful to:

- Meet someone who can further your cause (job search)
- Learn more about the industry, company, and/or job you are interested in
- Hear more about a current or future job opportunity
- Be introduced to a decision maker or someone else who can influence your candidacy once you apply for a job
- Get you up to speed by serving as a resource or mentor when you make a change in industry

What follow are some guidelines for getting the most from your informational interviews. After conducting a few of these, interviewing for actual jobs later on will be much easier and make you feel more comfortable. A side benefit of doing informational interviews during your research, networking, and/or career exploration is that you will learn the lingo—the current terminology or language used for the industry. This will enable you to speak more like an insider during your interviews, sounding smart and prepared. Also, from the informational interviews you will start to gain a sense of the energy, the vibe, the pace, the big picture, and the nuances of the industry. These will be helpful in determining how you should prepare for and position yourself when you start to interview for jobs.

Set an Agenda

Know what you want to achieve with your informational interviewing. You should focus on three main objectives:

1. Make a connection with an individual in an industry, organization, or kind of job function that you are interested in.
2. Research the field/industry, job function, and organization.
3. Help you develop your next steps.

Make the first contact. Contact the person you are asking for an interview. Introduce yourself briefly. Let the individual know who referred you and ask for about 15 minutes of his time. Arrange a time to speak by telephone, in person, or in an IM (instant messaging) session.

If you are less familiar with the person you'll be approaching, take a bit more formal approach. Send a letter requesting an informational interview and indicate who referred you or how you thought of the person. Note that you are including your résumé so that the person can get a quick sense of your background and abilities. Wait a week or so, and then follow up with a telephone call or an e-mail. Ask if the individual has received your information (if not, you'll have to summarize briefly) and reiterate your request for an informational interview, about 15 minutes of her time at her convenience.

Set a date and time. If the person agrees, then schedule a time to talk and ask if she prefers you come to the office or call. If you are talking by telephone, offer to call the person and confirm the best number to call. For instance, on that date, you may need to call a cell phone or ring an assistant who will connect you.

Prepare your list of questions ahead of time. The next section includes ideas for questions that will help you probe for the information you need. The questions earlier in this chapter on researching industries and companies are also useful to reference.

Conducting the Interview

Respect the person's time. When you conduct the interview, start off by saying that you want to be sensitive to time so you will start right in with the questions if that is okay. Begin with a few easy ones, such as the person's background and how she got into the industry or company; what the individual likes or doesn't like about the job or the organization; the biggest changes over the time the person has faced in the company or the industry.

Convey, don't curb, your enthusiasm. Throughout your time together, show interest, enthusiasm, and appreciation. Be an active listener. Take notes so you remember what was said and can refer to them later. Honor the time commitment. It is up to the person if she wants to extend the time with you.

Go out on a limb. Toward the end of the conversation, if your discussion has gone well and the person is responsive and helpful, go out on a limb and ask for three things:

1. Feedback, especially constructive, on your fit and your chances of making a move into the industry and/or company. Ask for suggestions for how you can you improve your candidacy in general—what can you do to be more competitive?
2. Recommendations of a few colleagues who might have job opportunities in your area of interest or who might be willing to speak with you, even informationally.
3. Permission to touch base with the individual periodically. Ask the person to do the same, especially if she hears about opportunities or thinks about other information that would be helpful to you.

Show genuine appreciation. After the interview, thank the individual enthusiastically for giving you the time. Genuinely show her your appreciation and follow up with a handwritten thank-you note within three or four days. If the person really went above and beyond to help you and your budget allows, follow up with a thoughtful gesture: Send flowers, a book, or tickets to a concert or sporting event or something the person would enjoy. The key point is to personalize the thank-you.

In summary, keep these dos and don'ts in mind for your informational interviews:

Dos	Don'ts
Be purposeful with your time	Take a contact for granted
Be thoughtful and professional	Have a defeatist attitude
Treat each contact like a client	Let a "no" or rejection stop you
Be respectful of the person's time	Be afraid to ask for other referrals
Be genuine in your thanks	Forget to reciprocate to; help others

A list of starter questions for your informational interviewing is included at the end of this chapter.

● TOOLS AND RESOURCES

Frequently Asked Interview Questions

What interests you in our organization?

Why do you want this job?

What do you know about us—what concerns you, what do you think you like?

Why do you deserve this job versus all the other people I'm interviewing?

What motivates and inspires you? What would demotivate you?

Tell me something about yourself that would surprise me.

Overview the key steps in your career; tell me the thing you are most proud of accomplishing in each; explain why you made your next move.

What would your previous managers say if I asked them to tell me about you?

What would your peers or colleagues say about you?

What would your staff—those who have reported to you directly—say about you?

What would your mom or dad tell me about you?

Describe yourself in five adjectives.

What are your strengths?

Everyone has areas he or she wants to or needs to develop; what are yours?

What do you see yourself doing in the next few years? How about further along?

Tell me in one sentence, when you look back on your career, what do you want to have accomplished?

Tell me about a time that you failed and what you learned.

Describe a situation in which you took a risk.

Give me an example of a time you had to learn something fast.

Tell me about a time you had to implement an idea.

Share an example of a time when you had to persuade others to do something.

Tell me about a time when you had to juggle many competing priorities, lots of projects, or many activities all at once.

Who else are you interviewing with?

What's your evaluation and decision process for how you'll choose among offers (if you have more than one)?

What have I not asked you about that you think I should know about you?

Behavioral Interviewing: What to Expect

A particular genre of interviewing—*behavioral interviewing*—has been used by recruiters since the 1980s and is still a popular approach used today. Familiarizing yourself with this approach will provide helpful preparation for your interviews.

The premise of behavioral interviewing is that past behavior is the best predictor for future behavior or success. Rather than basing questions on trait theory (tell me about your creativity or how are you hardworking?) or hypotheticals (what would you do if _____? or how would you handle _____?), behavioral interviewing is based on an individual's past actions and behaviors. What have you actually experienced and how? What did you do? How did you behave or act that would prove to be a good indicator of what you would do, how you would behave or act in the future?

Behavioral-interview questions typically start with phrases such as:

- "Give me an example of a time when you _____"
- "Describe an experience in which you _____"
- "Tell me about a situation that you used _____"

Some common fill-ins for the blanks are:

- Worked in a team
- Led or initiated something
- Used your creativity

- Mastered or learned something quickly
- Adapted to a change
- Asked for forgiveness, not permission
- Took a risk
- Made a mistake
- Did something out of the ordinary
- Solved a complex problem
- Multi-tasked
- Negotiated with or influenced others
- Were conflicted ethically
- Ran with the ball
- Overcame an obstacle
- Dealt with a crisis
- Learned something that surprised you
- Overcame resistance or negativity
- Assimilated and made sense out of a large amount of data
- Displayed organizational skills
- Handled a lot of pressure, juggling priorities and competing deadlines

Interviewing Dress Rehearsal

To get some valuable practice that will help build stronger interviewing skills, try this dress rehearsal. After you have prepared key points and thoughts for your answers, run through an interview from start to finish as you would a dress rehearsal for an important performance or presentation. Follow the steps below:

1. Set aside 25 minutes and review the first five FAQs (frequently asked questions). Jot down on a piece of paper, in a journal, or on your computer the key points and thoughts you would include in your answers. Practice a few times articulating out loud what you would say. Each time try to incorporate the key points and thoughts and sound at ease with the words you are expressing.
2. Another day, set aside 25 minutes and review the next five FAQs. Repeat the instructions in #1 above.

3. When you have completed all of the FAQs, as extra practice, ask a friend or colleague to serve as your interviewer and simulate an interview. Ask the friend to randomly choose from the list of questions and throw you some curveballs (questions not on the list) as well. Dress how you would for the interview, and ask the friend to do the same. Walk through the interview from start to finish, including handshakes, eye contact, and all. If you need more practice, rehearse again, next time videotaping the interview.

When It's Your Turn to Ask the Interviewer

When the interviewer or recruiter asks if you have any questions, have some all ready to use, like those that follow. Depending on time, you would probably ask only a few.

"Could you tell me about your background and career path?"

"How did you come to join the company?"

"What do you like most about your colleagues? Your work?"

"Tell me something about the CEO and senior team that's not easy to glean from your recruiting literature, Web site, etc."

"How does someone succeed and do well in your organization? What are the critical success factors?"

"What's the best thing about the company? The worst thing?"

"What have you learned about your job or the company that has surprised you?"

"What's the best advice you have for someone wanting to work for your organization?"

"What's your recruiting timeline and process for this job?"

"Based on what we discussed, what challenges, issues, or concerns do you have about my being the best for this job? I'd like to address those now if I may."

Informational Interviewing: A Starter List of Questions

Choose from the following list of questions depending on how much time you have with the person you are interviewing. Add to the list with your own questions or adapt these to better fit your style and needs:

"What's your background?"

"How did you get your start in the industry?"

"What do you like best and least about your job?"

"How would you approach a job search for this company, industry, or field?"

"What advice do you have for someone trying to get into the industry or field?"

"What's the company culture like that only an insider might know?"

"Describe a week or a day in your job."

"What companies are growing and hiring right now?"

"What ideas do you have to learn about where the job opportunities are?"

"What are the best ways to research and keep updated on the industry—for example, the best periodicals or journals, special interest groups, etc.?"

"What are the hot spots for meeting people in the field—specific conferences, trade shows, watering holes, charity events, in a park on the weekend, or at a game of beach volleyball every Saturday in the summer?"

"Could you give me some feedback on how I can make myself a stronger contender for a job in this industry or field?"

"Given my background, what could I do short term to make myself a stronger candidate?"

"Could you recommend other colleagues with whom I can speak? Is it okay to use your name when I contact them?"

"Could I call or e-mail you from time to time to ask your advice or to see if I'm moving in the right direction?"

Additional Resources for Interviewing Effectively

For more advice and insights about interviewing, refer to my Web site, www.career-inspirations.com, and read these specific articles:

- *Surviving and Thriving in a Tough Job Market: Acing Your Interviews.* This is a Top Ten list of tips for preparing for and performing most effectively in your interviews.

- *Ten Executives Tell What They Look for in Interviews.* These include Heather Killen, SVP of worldwide operations for Yahoo!; Wes Smith, COO of Del Monte Foods; John Helding, senior director of worldwide recruitment for Booz, Allen, & Hamilton Consulting; Louis Armory, partner for Bain & Co.; and Jim Bierne of General Mills.
- *When It's Your Turn to Ask Questions.* This includes more questions you might ask your interviewers.
- *Decoding the Interviews.* This discusses the taxonomy of an interview (the stages and components), how to read body language and other cues from the recruiter, and how employers usually evaluate candidates (evaluation criteria, how interviewer feedback on the candidates is gathered and used, the decision-making process for which candidates get the yes, no, or maybe/put on hold).

Recharging a Job Search That Is Dragging On

HAVE YOU BEEN in your job search much longer than you hoped for or anticipated? Does your job search seem to be dragging on? Are you losing your
energy, focus, or momentum? How about feeling hopeless or kind of down?
Are you short on job and networking leads? Has it been difficult to uncover
where the jobs are, especially the hidden job market? Have you tried most
everything you can think of and read or applied the first four chapters to
looking for a job, but nothing is getting your job search moving, much less
in high gear?

● DEFINING THE CHALLENGE

If your job search is dragging on, there are two most likely reasons: (1) you
are not generating enough job leads, in which case you've got to start digging even deeper, expanding your networking, and exploring new avenues
for job possibilities; or (2) you are losing steam, which slows your momentum, causes your motivation to wane, and negatively affects how you are
coming across in your interviews and when meeting recruiters. Maybe you
feel tired, beaten down, and unenthusiastic, and it shows.

● FACING THE CHALLENGE

For a job search that is dragging on, this chapter will help you. First, you'll
find out how to rejuvenate your job search with new contacts, directions,
and leads. Then, we'll discuss creative ideas, offering boosts of inspiration

and practical advice for going from puttering along to revving up your job search.

Generate More Job and Networking Leads

Pump up your informational interviewing. Take a look at the previous chapter on interviewing, particularly the section on conducting informational interviews. If your job search is dragging on, one way to pick up the pace and generate more job leads is to pump up the volume on your informational interviewing. Commit to doing *at least* two or three informational interviews a week, preferably in person but also by telephone.

Informational interviews are especially useful when you don't have a large network of your own or you have already utilized your network with few results. Although these interviews are not for actual jobs, they do glean valuable information and contacts that can lead you to jobs. Informational interviews effectively expand your network and connect you with people who are actually working in the industries and companies you are targeting. They also generate viable referrals to people who are hiring and help you feel more comfortable in your actual interviews.

Finding new sources. Basically, an informational interview means that you identify people in your targeted industries, companies, and organizations, or a particular job function, field, or profession. There are many sources for identifying people to interview. Your current network is the best place to start. This is an easy, low-involvement way for your friends and family to assist you. If you don't have a network or it hasn't really been useful for you, try these five other sources for networking and obtaining informational interviews:

1. Start with organizations and people you are connected to. You already know or can easily meet people from your school's alumni association and local chapters or religious, social, and volunteer affiliations. Take a look at the business cards or your contact database or rosters for the names you've collected over the last year. These could include people you met at professional conferences, seminars, or trade shows; while volunteering for a charity event, or someone in your reading club, sports

team, new moms' group, and so on. Contact two or three of them and see if you can get together for something like coffee, lunch, or a walk that will let you further the relationship.

Additionally, find out what programs or activities these organizations have planned. Try to participate in at least one per week. Volunteer to take registration, help set up an event, or do something that will put you in contact with lots of people. Set a goal for yourself to meet 5 to 10 new people at each event. Bring your business cards that include your name and contact information.

2. Try some new networking organizations. These include your local chamber of commerce, your city's Toastmaster's Club, and more specialized organizations like First Tuesday, a network for innovation and technology that operates in 36 cities and 19 countries on five continents.

3. Contact a few people you admire. Perhaps you recently have read in the news about someone whom you respect. Maybe there are a few illustrious alumni from the schools you've attended or someone you know of through your volunteer work or social activities. Contact them, let them know why you admire them, and explain that you would appreciate their insights on a career change you are thinking about. People whom we tend to admire, although busy, are often generous and giving. If they can offer some advice via e-mail or a quick 15 to 20 minutes over coffee, they will.

4. Volunteer for something new. Offer your time and talents to a new cause or group. This could be for a nonprofit organization, your city government, your community, or something purely interesting or fun. Examples include food kitchens, a homeless shelter, literacy or world peace programs, an arts-related community event, or an event such as an art and wine festival or Earth Day celebration.

5. Find out a company's pet causes. If you have a list of companies you are interested in, look on their Web sites, search your local newspaper, or talk with someone in each company's community relations group to find out what charities or specific causes they support. Do a search on the particular charity or cause on Yahoo! or Google and see what upcoming big events or fund-raisers they are organizing. Get involved in helping out. This will more than likely put you directly in contact with employees from the companies you are targeting.

Do It Yourself

Make your own job. One way to generate more job leads that you might not have even considered is to start working for yourself. At a minimum, you could do this until you find something else. Working for yourself will keep your skills sharp and your mind engaged, build up your experience, and bring in some money. The people you meet through your work are excellent sources of jobs (actual or referrals), too.

The easiest way to make your own job is to take an expertise or strength you have and find clients who can use it. Check out Web sites such as guru.com, freeagent.com, or the Small Business Administration for ideas and leads. Your old companies and their clients (if you are not bound by noncompetition agreements) are possibilities. Some creative ways to offer something and uncover new sources of clients follow.

- *Fill an unmet need.* If there are people, groups, or companies and organizations that you know need something but perhaps it is too expensive for them, inefficient, or not cost-effective, think about what you can offer. For example, small companies might not be able to have a full-time employee to perform functions like recruiting, accounting, payroll, PC/network support, or office cleaning. If you have the experience or know-how, then offer your services.
- *Follow a dream.* If there was something you have always wanted to do and have shown some talent for it, now is the time to try it. For example, maybe you love animals. Why not take a dog-training course through your local humane society or apprentice with some respected animal behaviorists or veterinarians in your area. From there you could start a dog-sitting, training, or day-care service. Maybe you love animals *and* photography. Become a photographer specializing in pets. Work with some pet boutiques or stores to come in once a month or around the holidays and offer affordable pet photography.
- *Use a gift you already have.* If you are often complimented on your ability to pull an outfit together or serve as a wonderful host/hostess or as the world's best baker of cookies, think about starting your own business as a stylist, event or wedding planner, or cookie baker selling to some restaurants or specialty stores. You need to start with only one paying client. If

you're good or great, then word of mouth will spread your reputation fast. The possibilities really are endless but are bound by your financial situation and risk profile.

- *Go back to the future.* Restart an old friendship that has faded with time. Go back to your past and draw on it to move you forward into your future. Who were the managers, the colleagues, or staff members in your past work experiences whom you respected or really enjoyed working with? Reconnect with those people.

  Many of your old work friends and colleagues will have changed to different organizations; some may have switched into different fields or industries. That is even better because it means they represent a broader network of connections. You may be able to find them by doing a Google search. Or do it the old-fashioned way via the telephone book or by contacting someone you know who would have remained in touch. Your former colleagues may not have specific jobs for you, but at minimum, reconnecting with them will give you an energy boost. At best, they may be a font of information for companies that are or will be hiring. They can also refer you to their friends and colleagues.

- *Do the sequel.* Going back to the future could also mean that you may wind up going back to work for a previous employer. Maybe you try for a different function or group so it's more interesting for you. There are some advantages to returning to a past employer. People there know your track record. If you did not burn your bridges when you left, they will be more likely to give you a chance to try something new—a new job in a different group from the one you were in before—that is more aligned with your current interests. You will also have the benefit of knowing the culture, the players, and the business. This should enable you to come in and perform well quickly.

- *Be true to your school.* There is something uniquely special about contributing—giving back in some way—to your school. For most of us, mention of our school brings back wonderful memories of a close-knit community and interesting, stimulating people. On their part, schools always appreciate alumni involvement. For example, many MBA programs hire alumni for key roles—career management, admissions, development, alumni relations, corporate relations, even IT (information technology).

  Explore ways in which you can use your strengths and experience to contribute to your school. Start by doing your homework on the school's Web site if you have not kept up with what's been going on. Get a feel for the current state of the school, its top priorities, any significant changes since you were a student. Find out what the dean values and sees as top challenges.

Call a professor, an administrator, the head of the career services center, or one of the deans who knows you. Seek the individual's insights on what initiatives and priorities the school is working on. Update the person on your background and brainstorm for ideas on where you could be of use. Ask for names to refer your résumé to and help open some doors for you. Express your avid interest in contributing to the school.

Uncover the Hidden Job Market

Play sleuth. What companies are actually growing? Which are doing well or tracking toward becoming stars in their industry? Which companies have filed numerous patents? Which are expanding internationally? What companies are hiring like crazy, with lots of job postings on their Web sites or advertising in the Sunday job ads?

Make a Top Ten list of companies that are a match with what you want. Research them, visit their Web sites, and look up their employment opportunities. Network in through anyone you know to talk with someone—anyone—in the company. Branch out and build from there with your persistence and enthusiasm. If you don't know anyone, then take a chance and write to the CEO or some alumni from your school.

Find out who is leaving their jobs. Join a career action group or job search or networking group. These groups are offered through your church, synagogue, parish, or religious organization, your school's alumni association, a career coach or career center, an industry or professional association, or the like. If you can't unearth any groups this way, do an Internet search. Try Yahoo! or Google and type in the key words: "job search groups," "career networking," or "networking groups." Join a group. Chances are some of the people in the group have just left an organization you are interested in. They will have fresh contacts and intimate knowledge about their former organizations, such as who is hiring, where the jobs are, and how to get your foot in the door.

Keep Up Your Job Search Momentum

If your focus and energy are waning, try these tips and strategies to regain your momentum and get yourself up to speed in your job search.

Celebrate your wins. Pat yourself on the back for what you have accomplished so far. Identify your wins. Maybe one win was that you followed up on several promising leads. Perhaps you are close to an offer or just got a call back for further interviews. Maybe you are gaining more confidence in your interviewing skills. Whether the win is small or big, be grateful and thank yourself for what you achieved.

Reflect and revise. Think about what you've done on your job search to date. Focus on two things that you could improve on. Could you have a better job search plan? Faster thank-you letters following interviews? How about being more prepared to ask the recruiter questions? Or could you be stronger in how you go about sourcing job leads?

Do your spring cleaning. Think specifically about what you've been doing that is not working for you anymore. When you are cleaning out your closet or desk drawers, you get rid of things that you don't need or use. Likewise in your job search, are there behaviors, attitudes, or activities that are not doing you any good? If the answer is yes, figure out what they are and get rid of them. Edit them out. For example, have you been going to a specific counselor or a career action support group that hasn't been helpful? Stop going. Is your current résumé not eliciting a positive response? Get a makeover. Review Chapter 3 for ideas. Do you consistently have great interviews until the final phase? Figure out what you've been doing wrong and stop doing it. Are you negotiating in an antagonistic way, or are you overconfident? Eliminate that behavior.

Cry on someone's shoulder. It may be the case that you need emotional support or a friendly ear. Call or get together with a friend who is a great listener. Tell your friend about what is bothering you. Remember to reciprocate when you can.

Shake it up. Are your short-term goals and priorities still realistic? Is it time to consider contingency plans B or C, or even taking a completely different direction? Try a new path. Change directions. Attempt a new approach or different perspective. Get out of your rut. Shake off your inertia. Even a small change can net you big results. Ideas can include going to your plan B industry or set of companies, thinking about project work versus full-time while you are still looking, or moving to another city that has intrigued you, especially if more jobs are available there.

Fan the flames. For every interview you've had that you think went well—but have not had a response or even got turned down on—systematically call or e-mail those recruiters or managers. Tell them you were sorry things didn't work out at that time. Let them know of your continued interest. Ask them to keep you in mind for the future. And find out if there are any questions they have or if you can provide further information. Keep connected and stay in touch. There are many times when someone who got an offer doesn't accept and the opening is available again. Often it's the candidates who are top-of-mind who get a second chance.

Forget about it. Take a mental break from your job search. Don't think or do anything about it for a day, a few days, even a week. Instead, do something you love and that makes you happy. Take a road trip with friends, play volleyball, cheer up the residents of a senior center, barbecue for your family, go to a spa, watch your favorite DVDs, tinker with your car. Engage yourself in what will rejuvenate and inspire you. This will give you a boost of energy for jumping back into your job search.

Keep the faith. Remember what makes you unique. Think about what you are good at and how you are good. Reflect on a quality or two that you are most proud of. Appreciate all of your talents and strengths. Everyone has them. If you can't think of any of yours, ask a friend, an old teacher, a colleague who thinks you're great, your partner, or your mom or dad to remind you of what they are. Realize that work is just one dimension in your total life vision. Your career is a long journey with many twists and turns along an unknown path. Your work, job, or career is not who you are in total. It is one vital part of a whole that is pretty darn special. Keep believing in yourself and your abilities and don't let yourself get down.

● TOOLS AND RESOURCES

Use the worksheet in Figure 5-1 to expand and diversify your contacts for networking. Starting with a few can result in many more.

Figure 5-1. Five Contacts Can Produce Twenty Additional Contacts

Names of Friends or Business Contacts	1. .... ⬇	2. .... ⬇	3. .... ⬇	4. .... ⬇	5. .... ⬇
Their Friends or Business Contacts					

Starting a New Job

ARE YOU A LITTLE NERVOUS about starting your new job with a new employer, a new group of colleagues, or in a new career, project, or role? Have you just joined a new company and are wondering how to put your best foot forward? Are you unsure about how to decode your new environment, integrate with the people and culture, and set yourself up for success?

It's very natural to feel anxiety about something unknown or uncertain. It's like you are a performer and are experiencing butterflies in your stomach. No matter how hard you've worked up until this point in your career, you are having those opening night jitters because you care so much about the venture you are about to embark on. Your job matters to you. You want to do your best and show your "audience" your most capable and vital performance.

● DEFINING THE CHALLENGE

There is a lot to keep in mind and to prepare for when you are about to start a new job. We've all witnessed what can go wrong and it's not pretty. New hires come into a new organization. They bring impressive backgrounds and lots of potential. Somehow they get off on the wrong foot or get sidetracked. Perhaps they never quite fit in with the culture, rubbed key people the wrong way, were arrogant, or fatally misjudged what was expected of them. Maybe, unbeknownst to them, they got caught in the crossfire of company politics. Whatever their faux pas, the aftermath was that

71

their careers in their new organizations derailed. In a sense, they failed to remember their basics, to move from their core (their strengths), to listen and learn about their new environment, and then to stay in step with others. Their missteps most likely ended with their leaving the organization at some point or being asked to leave.

This is the harsh reality, but the fact is that you are an unknown. Coming into a new situation, a new job, or a new role, you will be judged. No matter how supportive the organization's culture, no matter how warm and wonderful the people, you will be viewed and evaluated 360 degrees. Human nature dictates that the people you are working with—your manager, colleagues, and direct reports (if you have staff)—will all form initial impressions of you. Your competence, how well you fit in, what you can do for them, and how much time and energy they should invest in you and the relationship are being assessed. Others you will interact with, such as clients, strategic partners, and vendors, also will be "sizing you up." In the time-stretched, fast-paced, uncertain work environments of our times, this quick evaluation inevitably happens.

● FACING THE CHALLENGE

The good news is that you can create your own masterful performance and garner rave reviews early on. To deal with starting a new job effectively, you need to know what to watch out for and how to prepare for the smoothest transition. You need to choreograph your entry strategy and focus on what you need to do to get off to a graceful, strong start. This is especially crucial in the first 90 days.

You can manage many of the aspects of starting a new job so that you are the most successful you can be. None of us is perfect and there will be some bumps or big potholes in the road. The key is to do much more well than wrong, overall. This chapter tells you what to look out for and what you need to do to get started on the right foot.

Adapting to Your New Environment

Learn the lay of the land. Do a lot of observing and listening the first week or so. Of course, speak up and engage when you need to, but stop, look, and listen. Get to know your new landscape. Who are the key players? How do people work together? What seems to be valued in the organization? What are the hot buttons, the warm issues, and the high priorities?

Watch out for common missteps. You can be forgiven for your early slip-ups, but why spend time digging yourself out of a hole when you can sidestep mistakes altogether? Here's a list of some common mistakes people make when starting a new job. Identify any others you can think of for your own situation:

- Violating company policy without realizing it
- Misinterpreting how critical something is and missing a crucial deadline
- Debating or being overaggressive versus discussing a topic in a group meeting
- Challenging a higher-up or someone else you shouldn't until you get to know the person better
- Upgrading to first-class travel or asking for some special treatment when there's a formal process for requesting these perks or you have to earn them somehow
- Declining invitations to go out for lunch or after work with a group, thus being considered standoffish
- Coming in late, wearing the wrong thing, or engaging in excessive personal phone calls
- Sending out an extremely long e-mail to too many people versus going to talk to a few core people
- Criticizing the company's new ad campaign, new product launch, and so on

Clues on missteps usually can be found in your company's Employee Guide or Handbook. The best way to learn these fast, however, is to ask a few people who have been in the company a while. Go to those who seem respected, knowledgeable, and willing to help the new kid on the block. Call on a few of those you have gotten to know well in the recruiting process. Ask them, "What mistakes should someone new try to avoid?" "What are the big transgressions someone could make unintentionally that might impact his or her career?" In knowledge there is power. The power is to keep these missteps in the back of your mind and be aware not to make them.

Respect the core values and the culture. Go beyond the espoused values and culture. Immerse yourself in the organization as best you can. Get to know, listen to, and observe those around you, particularly those in leadership roles and those who are well respected. Watch their actions to see what is truly valued.

For deciphering the culture, mostly you will just need to be in it for a while. Be cognizant of cues such as:

- How people communicate and disagree
- Why people get recognized or rewarded
- What happens when a deadline is missed or someone fails
- How managers treat their employees
- How everyone treats customers
- How competition, teamwork, consensus are viewed
- Who the keepers of the culture are—those who carry the torch for upholding the culture

Pay attention to context. Listen to what is being said, but also hear what is not being said. Use your instincts and intuition to read between the lines. If this is not a talent of yours, find someone you can trust. Take the person aside and ask her to give you the take on something you think has more meaning than on the surface. Ask the person to help you figure out what just happened or if there is an undercurrent to what was just said.

Get to know the communication norms. How do people communicate both formally and informally, verbally and nonverbally? How does important information get shared? Is your new organization an e-mail or voice mail place or is it a talk-in-person type of culture?

Cultivate key relationships. Treat every interaction with someone new as a chance to learn about him, what he does, and how that fits into the greater whole. Find out what's on people's minds, especially any past problems they have had with the person in your job. Get to know Human Resources (HR). This group manages the people "processes" but more important, they can be valuable advocates in your career development and coaching. Build ties with your manager and core group of colleagues. Take time to get to know their backgrounds, their motivations, their special skills and abilities, and their pet peeves.

Fitting In

Get in synch with your manager. If your manager has not mentioned formally sitting down with you to discuss things, ask for an informal orientation and some regular touch-base meetings the first few months to help you get up to speed as quickly as possible. Find out about the important aspects of your job and the relationship with your manager. These include management style, preferred way to communicate, biggest challenges and priorities for the group, your own goals and objectives. Let your manager know that you are eager to learn and that you appreciate feedback on how you are doing as well as how you can improve.

Be clear on your critical success factors. What do you need to do to succeed in your role? What are the critical success factors? What are your goals and objectives within the first 90 days, six months, and first year?

Identify your "go-to" people. Learn who the gatekeepers in the organization are. These are the "go-to" people who always seem to be in the know. They are like wise sages and are typically willing to help others and share what they know. Remember that the most respected and powerful people are not necessarily those with the titles. The person who delivers the mail, a VP's assistant, the company café manager, and the receptionist can be highly revered and liked, with their opinions or what they say holding a lot of weight.

Know whom to watch out for. Find out who the people are that you should be careful around. Unfortunately, in every organization, there are those who gossip, are negative, or like to see others fail.

Newbie Be Good

Use your newness to your advantage. Realize that your first 60 days or so offer a prime opportunity to use your fresh perspective to come up with new ideas, devise creative solutions, or share your different point of view. Choose strategically what you will tackle or engage in, but by all means leverage your newbie status to do what good you can. Also, if you do happen to make some mistakes early on, acknowledge them quickly and honestly. Say you are sorry you didn't know, but make sure to learn from the situations. Those you are working with will cut you some slack for a while. Being new can be used as a valid excuse in moderation.

Achieve some small wins early on. You don't have to hit the ball out of the park on the first pitch, but do give the extra effort to make progress on your goals and objectives. Outside of your job responsibilities, if there are immediate ways you can contribute and make a difference, whether on a project, to solve a problem, or to contribute to a group discussion, do this as much and as often as you can. Creating some concrete wins or achieving some accomplishments early on can help to set a vibrant stage for your future.

Help other new people who come after you. The best way to keep learning is to teach others. You remember what starting up your new job was like; it's still fresh in your mind. Extend your lessons learned and insights to others who are joining the organization. Become a formal or informal mentor to someone new. Offer your services to Human Resources to assist with recruiting or the new hire orientations. Provide constructive feedback based on your recent experiences, including solutions for bringing new people in and getting them up and running as quickly as possible.

● TOOLS AND RESOURCES

Before You Start Your Job: A Checklist

❏   Choose in advance what outfit you will wear and your accessories. Getting those kinds of details out of the way and wearing

something that you feel confident and comfortable in are important to making a good impression on your first day.

❏ Re-read your job description or review what you and your manager discussed about overall expectations.

❏ Review any company literature or notes from your research and
interviews to remember key names and players: your CEO, people in your group if you've met them, the Human Resources director or recruiter with whom you've interviewed, etc.

❏ Be prepared to answer the same questions about yourself many
times over the first few weeks: where you went to school or
where you worked before, what you did, how you like it in the
company so far, etc. Both a basic 10-second and a longer 2-
minute spiel about yourself are good to have ready.

❏ Arrive to work early on your first day and relax a bit before you
get going.

❏ Bring a few things to make your office or workspace your own:
a few photos, some desk gadgets, your favorite paperweight, a
plant.

Working for a Bad Boss

IS YOUR BOSS SOMEONE who demotivates or demoralizes you? Is nothing you do ever good enough? Do you have a boss who yells or throws tantrums when things don't go his way? Are you working for someone who is moody as if on an emotional roller coaster—one day she is cheery and friendly, the next day she is downright mean? Does your boss take credit for your work or play favorites or worry only about his own career? Is your manager someone whom you just don't respect? Is your boss a negative role model—an example of someone whom you do *not* want to be like when you manage others?

● DEFINING THE CHALLENGE

Having a bad boss is a major problem no matter how much you may like your actual job, your company, or your coworkers. A bad boss can mean many different things depending on what's important to you and how you like to be managed. The bottom line is that a bad boss is someone with whom you don't do your best work or someone you dread seeing when you go to work. A bad boss is someone you don't respect and you probably don't like as a person, either.

When I've worked with managers who need coaching and development because of low morale on their staffs, bad marks for their management skills, formal complaints, or negative feedback in exit interviews, I've found that the negative traits they possess are diverse. Bad bosses can be micromanagers, bullies, incompetents, emotional wrecks, absentees (never around when you need them), meanies, weanies (weak), or overambitious, take-all-the-credit types. They may be those managers who cannot make decisions, who play favoritism, who live constantly in crisis mode, or who are hypercritical.

● FACING THE CHALLENGE

If you are lucky, you have had your fair share of great bosses—those who have vision, lead by example, and take time to develop the people who work with them. These bosses are usually competent and motivating. They can make things happen, harness energy to set common priorities, and are respected by peers, higher-ups, and their staffs. In contrast, when you have a bad boss, the difference is glaring. This chapter discusses strategies, tips, and advice on how to cope with a bad boss.

Reality Check

Make sure you are not the problem. Look critically at yourself, how you behave, and your performance. Are you doing anything to cause or exacerbate the problem? For example, do you like to debate your boss or even goad him until he lashes out at you? Do you turn in your projects late and help create a crisis? Do you talk behind her back and tell anyone who will listen how awful she is? Are you experiencing personal problems that are making you unmotivated or unfocused even before you get to work?

Fix anything about yourself first. Get help if you need it—from a mentor either inside or outside the company, from professionals in your Human Resources department or your Employee Assistance Program (EAP), or by talking things over with a friendly coworker who knows the ins and outs of the situation. If it's truly not you, and the responsibility is squarely on your boss, then read on.

Make a list and check it twice. Write down what is bothering you about your boss. Is it a one-time episode or truly an ongoing condition? If you are unsure if it's something you are doing, do more fact finding. Speak discretely with people you can trust who also interact with your boss. Are they having similar difficulties? Do they seem to be experiencing some of the same problems you are? What, if anything, have they done to help their situations?

What are the actions, the behaviors, the attitudes, or the management style that are the problem? For each specific thing bothering you, jot down a few concrete examples. These will be helpful in explaining to your boss or to HR if you have to later on.

For example, if you list "micromanages," you may note examples such as:

- "Tells me each time, although I have been doing them for years, what I should do and say in my on-campus recruiting presentations for our college and MBA recruiting."
- "Asked me to come up with a plan for the product launch in China and has come uninvited to each conference call with the team. Worse yet, she interrupts me and takes over most of the discussion."
- "Looks over my shoulder when I am at my computer and tells me what I am doing wrong."

If you have listed "bullies me and others," you may cite something like:

- "Yelled at me again at the staff meeting for doing something slightly out of sequence from the agenda."
- "Witnessed him disparaging another director, a peer, to his boss, bragging that he could run circles around him, do it better, etc."

Dealing with the Problem on Your Own

Think about possible solutions. If there are many problems with your boss, try to focus on a few of the worst ones to speak with him about. Before you ask for a meeting, spend some quality time thinking about solutions for each problem. Ideally, perhaps there is something each of you can do.

Consider the first example in the list above for the micromanager. Perhaps you could offer to show her your PowerPoint presentation a few weeks before you start your on-campus talks. If your boss has input or changes, maybe she could jot them down and you could incorporate the ones that will work. Another solution might be to give your boss evaluations from the other recruiting team members or the students you are presenting to. If they are excellent (high), your boss will know what a terrific job you are doing. If you don't do evaluations but instead have results that you are directly responsible for in your on-campus recruiting, those may suffice.

Have a powwow with your boss. Schedule some time with your boss. Find a conducive time when he will listen to feedback about your relationship. Don't try it when he's just come back from an intense three-week trip through Europe, is preparing for vacation, or has his hands full with something his own boss has dumped on him.

Opt for a win-win approach. It goes like this. You enjoy many aspects of your job and you like the organization. You want to work more effectively with your boss and have a better working relationship. There are some problems getting in the way of that. You want to bring them to her attention. Ideally, you two will create some solutions together. What can you each do?

Consider whether you can live with the situation. If your boss doesn't get it, won't accept it, or cannot change, consider if you can avoid her as much as possible, live with the problems, and concentrate on what is positive in your work.

Bringing in Reinforcements

Ask a mentor or someone else you trust for help. You can seek a mentor's advice or even intervention. You may not have a formal mentor but a mentor can simply be someone who has been in the organization a while, who is respected and wise, and who cares about you. This can be a tricky situation because your boss could be offended or retaliate if you go to someone over his head or bring your problems to one of his peers. You will have to have faith that the person whom you are confiding in and asking for help can be trusted. If you must approach more than one person, keep it to as few people as possible.

Usually if your boss is unbearable and you just cannot stand it any-more, you don't have a lot to lose anyway. Ideally, a mentor is someone senior to your boss and someone savvy and adept enough at the internal politics to figure out how she can help you rather than hurt you and your career. For example, your mentor may have a discrete heart-to-heart talk with your boss. Your mentor might apply some pressure to the boss to change or help your boss with something that is causing him to act that way, and so on.

Go to the boss's boss. Going to your manager's manager is extremely risky and potentially career-limiting. This is what we call doing an end run around your boss. It's not looked on too kindly by most people because they believe if you can do this to your boss, you could do it to them. Some look at going to the boss's boss as almost the ultimate betrayal. You need to assess a couple of things before you decide to do this. First, you'll need to determine if it can make the situation better and second, if the risks are worth it. For example, some possible risks are your being considered a backstabber, a whiner, or a betrayer; your manager finding out and retaliat-ing against you, making your work life even more hellish; or your being reassigned to a job you don't like or an even worse manager.

Answer these questions to assess whether you should go and have a talk with your boss's boss:

- Does your boss's boss know you and think highly of you? The best of all worlds is that your boss's boss knows your work, thinks you are great, and would not want the company to lose you.
- If the boss's boss doesn't know you, would she believe what you have to say? If yes, will she care enough to do something about the situation?
- What's the relationship between your boss and his boss? For exam-ple, are they such good buddies that you will not get an impartial "audience"?
- How important is your boss in the organization and how much power does he really wield? For example, is your boss so indispens-able to the organization that his boss or HR would look the other way no matter how bad a manager he is?

- What's the worst thing your boss could do if he found out you went to his boss? Realistically, what is the probability of your boss doing the worst thing?

Involve HR if needed. Talking with HR about your boss is another option for you, but it, too, can be risky. If your HR group is equitable (favors management and employees equally) and respects everybody as partners in the business, chances are that involving the group will help your situation. Involving HR means that your feedback on your boss will be "on the record." In other words, if your boss does start to retaliate after you have tried to work things out, HR will be cognizant of this. More important, HR professionals will know if others (employees or peers) in the organization have had similar problems with your boss. They will probably be privy to whether your boss is going through some tough personal or emotional times. HR will be sensitive, too, if your boss is having problems with his own boss. Although HR will not divulge this confidential information, it can take these aspects into consideration. The bigger picture—how your boss is, any history, and what is going on—will be helpful to HR as it gets involved.

Human Resources professionals are usually adept at handling situations with bad bosses, but the follow-up actions they take and the outcomes can vary widely. Usually HR will get involved when the staff has unusually low morale, there is a formal complaint against a manager, or there is a trend of negative exit-interview feedback from employees who worked with the manager. High-potential performers who may be lacking management skills but who are strong in other critical areas of the business may also get Human Resources intervention. This is most often focused development and coaching to become better managers, depending on where the individual needs it.

There are many cases where bosses have been talked with and "put on notice." They have made small attempts to change their behavior and that's been bearable enough. Sometimes bosses may eventually be let go if there have been enough reports of serious problems that they have been given many opportunities to correct. Sadly, there are also times when nothing is done about the bosses. HR may just be too busy or perhaps the group believes the employee is a "whiner" or someone who stirs up trouble. There are also situations in which the improvements are so painstakingly slow that the employee gets fed up and decides to leave.

The Last Resort

Be ready to walk. I often say that life is too short not to do work that you love. This includes the basic element of working with people that you truly enjoy and who stimulate and inspire you. If you have done everything you possibly can and your boss won't or can't change, it is time to consider leaving your job. This may mean getting a job with another company, but if you can move to another group in your company, go for it. You will need to have a strong track record of performance and others who may have to vouch for the fact that your boss, not you, is the problem.

If you think your boss will try to sabotage your move, then don't go through the normal process. Before you let your boss know that you are interviewing for a new job, bring your new boss in on what's been going on. Try to lock in the move (get the offer and accept it), and make sure you will have your new boss's support in getting you released from your current boss.

Your new boss, her higher up, or HR may actually need to step in to extricate or free you. It's not how you normally want to operate, but do get your ducks in a row. Do what you have to do to leave the situation. That doesn't mean trashing your boss. It does mean explaining enough so that your new boss knows why you want to transfer and that she may have to "do some battle" with your current boss to make that happen.

● TOOLS AND RESOURCES

Talking Points for Your Powwow

Try this exercise for preparing what you want to say and how you will say it for your meeting with your difficult boss:

- Review your list of facts about your observations and conclusions on your boss. If there are more than two or three, focus on only the top few.

- Write down or refine (if you already have them) specific examples of your boss's problem behavior. Think not only about recent events but also go back through the past few months.
- Draft the structure for your talk; think about how you will frame the problem(s), and write down some key points for what you will say.
- Role-play with a friend who will give you objective feedback on how you are coming across. You want to be professional, factual, firm, and composed. You don't want to be emotional, angry, threatening, or whining.
- Make adjustments. Tone it down, make it stronger, and so on, as needed.

Dealing with Difficult Colleagues

HAVE YOU EVER BEEN the topic of gossip among some of your colleagues? You see them talking in the employee café and their voices turn to whispers when you enter the room. Perhaps you heard a rumor about yourself that is completely untrue or found out that a colleague took credit for something you had done. Did you ever work with someone who complains constantly about everyone and everything? Have you been bothered by an overly friendly coworker who wants to get too personal, or by an overly aggressive one who raises her voice or starts yelling at you? What about a colleague who insists on telling you off-color or offensive jokes? Have you ever been forced to sit next to a coworker who smells as if he hasn't showered in days? Have you ever missed a deadline because someone didn't follow through on something the individual promised to do?

● DEFINING THE CHALLENGE

Having to regularly deal with difficult coworkers can wear you down, affect your job performance, and lower your morale. There is a wide range of bothersome behaviors that can create problems at work. The problems I have helped clients deal with are as diverse as the clients themselves, meaning they are all over the map. Different people will be annoyed, put off by, frustrated with, exasperated by, take offense at, or be unhappy about different actions or behaviors from their colleagues. Whatever the problem may be, you know when you are having a hard time dealing with a colleague.

● FACING THE CHALLENGE

The strategies and tips discussed in this chapter address problems of dealing with difficult colleagues, those within your immediate work group or department and those others you interact with frequently within your company. These can also be more broadly applied to people with whom you work outside your organization, such as vendors, strategic partners, clients, and colleagues from your volunteer activities.

We will take a look at the 10 most common problems with colleagues and offer strategies and tips on handling each of them.

● A TOP TEN LIST OF PROBLEMS AND SOLUTIONS

Gossiping

Gossip serves no purpose whatsoever in an organization. It's detrimental. It undermines trust, camaraderie, and productivity. Usually if colleagues gossip or start rumors, it's because they are insecure, are bored, feel threatened, or desperately need attention. Very rarely are these people evil or mean-spirited, although there are a few of those in every organization, unfortunately.

Nip it in the bud. If a coworker gossips to you, nip it in the bud. Do not encourage it. Don't engage in it. Try saying something like, "Oh, really?" then redirect the conversation back to business or something work related.

Check it out. If a coworker is gossiping about you, first make sure that you verify this fact with several trustworthy sources. If there are two or three well-intentioned, supportive colleagues who tell you or confirm for you that they have heard something from Jane Doe about you, find out what is. Then do yourself a favor and do something about it.

Talk with the gossiper. The best advice is to talk with the person directly in person or by telephone. Check your emotions at the door. Don't go in with a blaming or hostile attitude. Be cool, calm, and level-headed. Tell the individual you have heard from some sources you trust that she has been saying X, Y, and Z about you. Ask if this is true and hear what she has to say about it. If she fesses up, you may want to find out why she is passing along this gossip. For example, there are some people who consider gossip harmless. Maybe they came from a work group that encouraged it or maybe they think that gossip is just harmless chitchat with others.

Tell him to stop. Firmly ask the coworker to stop the gossiping immediately. If he doesn't, get your facts right. Compile what he has said, when, to whom, and the impact it has on you or your work. Talk with your manager, his manager, or HR about it. One of them should speak with him about it or, if warranted, it should become a performance issue.

Let it go. In some cases, letting the gossip go may be a viable option. If the gossiper, for example, is known for gossiping, or if people don't take what she says seriously, and if the gossiper is not respected, what she says is taken with a grain of salt. If the gossip doesn't really do you any material harm, then think about if the gossiper and the gossip are worth confronting.

Getting Too Personal

You don't have to be bosom buddies with your colleagues (unless you want to), but you do want a collegial, genial working relationship. When certain colleagues try to get too up-close and personal, asking questions, probing into your personal life, and wanting to socialize after work, try the following advice.

Set boundaries. Know the limitations of what you do and don't want to talk about or what you are willing or not willing to share. Know how much or how little you'd like to see people socially outside of work, if at all. Be gracious, but be firm.

For example, if a coworker is asking too many questions—for example, about your love life, your spouse, your children, your pay, health issues, a confidential project you are working on, or what really happened with your last employer—try the following strategy: Engage in the level of small talk you feel comfortable with. Perhaps you ask how his children are doing and in general tell him about yours or say about your pay that you always wish it could be more but feel it's fair for your background. Then either get back to work, walk away if you need to, or change the subject. If the problem continues and the coworker does not take your hints, tell him that you try to keep your personal life personal. Say that you're sure he's not trying to make you feel uncomfortable but his questions are doing just that. Ask that you keep your interactions work focused—that you would appreciate that.

If a colleague wants to go out to lunch occasionally and you're comfortable with it, that's one thing. But if a coworker wants to go out to lunch every day and you don't want to, give him a good, brief reason why you can't. Examples are: "I have so much work to catch up on and will be eating at my desk." "I'm trying to leave early today and not going out to lunch."

Backstabbing

This is the behavior that I consider the most unforgivable and reprehensible from a coworker. I define backstabbing as a deliberate action that a coworker takes without your knowledge, with the intention of doing harm to you or your career.

Examples of backstabbing are:

- Starting a rumor, such as that you're an alcoholic or have a drug problem, are having marital problems, or are sleeping with the boss.
- Undermining you or sabotaging your work. This could include deliberately making you seem incompetent or self-motivated in a team meeting; making you the butt of jokes or belittling you in front of your staff or boss; causing friction between you and another coworker; or beating you to the punch on something that was your responsibility or high-profile project.
- Saying something to your face but knowingly doing the exact opposite. This could be promising something to you, such as "you will be the first to know," "you can depend on getting this from me before your deadline," etc. while knowing full well that it will not happen. Or this could be flattering you and complimenting you all the time, then saying negative things about you to all others.

Advice for handling backstabbing from colleagues is as follows:

Make reasonably sure that the backstabbing is a fact. Discreetly talk with people you trust. Tell them you've heard some rumors going around about you, and ask if they have heard them, too. Try to track backwards and find the source. To be reasonably sure, I'd suggest confirming the backstabbing or backstabber with at least three independent sources.

Confront the backstabber. Depending on the seriousness of what the person is saying or doing behind your back, approach the backstabber. Suggest a meeting as soon as possible.

Be firm, factual, and calm. Tell the backstabber that you are concerned because it has come to your attention that there are some false rumors, or misinformation, or whatever going around about you. Let the backstabber know that several people have indicated him or her as the source.

Be quiet and see where it goes. Stay silent and let the backstabber talk. Tune into body language—for example, he or she looks away, fidgets, becomes very nervous, begins to perspire or blush in the face, and the voice shakes or changes pitch.

Assume the person will deny it. If someone is mean-spirited or desperate enough to backstab a colleague, then you have to think that the worst will happen—he or she will deny it. The backstabber will probably try to turn the tables on you such as saying that you are imagining things, you are paranoid or insecure, you have never liked him or her, or others have it in for the individual and told you incorrectly.

Put the backstabber on notice. By confronting the backstabber and letting him or her know that you know, you may be able to put a stop to the antics. If the person knows you know what has been going on, most often he or she will cease and desist.

Let it go. If the backstabber really dislikes you, is jealous, manipulative, mean-spirited, or worse, the person will probably not stop doing what he or she is doing. You can either let it go or take some offensive strategy. Letting it go means you forget about it and take the high road. Feel sorry for this person: What goes around comes around. If the backstabber is sending out negativity, it will come back to him or her somehow, some way.

Take offense. You can accept that you are not going to stop the person, but you can go on the offensive to minimize any impact, harm, or damage to your reputation, credibility, and ability to perform your job. An offensive strategy would include:

- *Let your contributions be known.* Let the people who matter to you and who are important to your career see for themselves the opposite of what the backstabber is saying. In other words, make sure you especially shine and negate what the backstabber has said by your actions, behavior, and accomplishments. For example, if the backstabber says you don't meet deadlines or are failing on a project, make sure people know you made the deadlines and know the success of your project. You don't have to overdo it or obsess about proving the backstabber wrong. Just make sure that on the key points of what the person is saying or doing to you, you prove the person wrong when you can. People will start to doubt what the person says, if they don't already.
- *Get others involved.* Discuss the situation with your manager to get her advice on how to handle it. Or talk to the person's manager and let that individual know what's going on. Say that you have tried to work it out with the person and just wanted make the manager aware. Send a brief e-mail or note to HR so it's on the record.
- *Be nice to the backstabber.* This approach shows you have class and are the bigger person.

Taking Credit for Your Work

When people take credit for your work or your idea, it's usually because they feel they are not being developed properly and need to get noticed. It could also be that the culture of the organization encourages competition, that someone can win but someone must lose. Sometimes someone is just not doing his job and may feel desperate to claim someone else's work as his own. Here are ways you can counteract someone taking credit for your work:

Don't hide your light under a blanket. You don't have to boast or brag, but do let people know about your significant accomplishments and good work. Make sure the people who count—those with whom you work, who make budget and resource decisions, or who have influence on your career— are aware of your accomplishments and your contributions. For example, if you don't have regular touch-base meetings with your boss, put together a weekly status report of what you've been working on, what you've achieved so far, and your progress toward the goal and/or deadline. Communicate to the organization in general about some big win, a huge achievement, or something critical accomplished; do this in ways that are acceptable (not considered bragging) to the organization.

Give others their due, but don't overdo it. Be generous about giving others credit when they deserve it, but be careful not to give it all away or not include yourself. I've known many high-potential managers, especially women, who were great about sharing the credit for a job well done but needed to be more watchful of overdoing this. In other words, they needed to be careful of always making it everyone else's contributions and not acknowledging their own roles in the success.

Negativity, Whining, or Constant Complaining

We're not talking about the occasional colleagues who commiserate, have a bad day and tell you about it, or call foul when something is wrong with the company, management, a policy, and so on. We are talking here about a coworker who can bring you down with a constant barrage of complaints, negativity, or whining about what's wrong with everyone and everything. These types of people see the glass half empty all the time; they believe the worst is always about to happen; they see the negative and bad in most everyone; they are energy vampires, draining you when you encounter them. There's not a whole lot you can do about these colleagues. They are usually genetically predisposed to this way of thinking or have become like this through years of experience and have baggage that you are not likely to make go away. The best advice is simple:

Avoid them. Stay away from the people who bring you down with their complaining and negativity. Don't volunteer for a committee with them. Try to work on projects and assignments that they won't be involved in. If you find yourself on a committee or project with them, stay away from them. Don't sit by them. Don't engage them in conversation. If they approach you, turn the other way or make an excuse to leave. Say you forgot your cell phone; you have a conference call in a minute; you see someone across the room whom you have to get an answer from, or the like.

Redirect them. If you must interact with such a person and he or she starts down a path of negativity or whining, then interrupt mid-sentence. Change the subject. Say his or her name to attract attention, such as: "Jim, we need to talk about _____." "Jennifer, I need to tell you this before I forget." "Jason, we are getting off track. We were supposed to be discussing _____."

Kissing Up

Most of us have encountered this type of colleague. They're the ones who ingratiate themselves to the boss, the CEO, and any other people they think can help their careers. They may tattle on their colleagues to the boss. They may agree with everything the boss or higher-ups say, flatter them insincerely, or compliment every idea as brilliant. This problem may be annoying, but the advice I have is brief.

Learn from their example. This is a good example of what not to do, how not to succeed, how not to be taken as sincere. Most senior managers or savvy people can see through the kissing up. Their egos may like what these people are saying or doing, but if they are good managers, they value performance, results, and employees who will tell it like it is, even if it's not pretty or pleasant.

The most fruitful business relationships are built on trust and respect. People who kiss up usually don't get either. We're not suggesting that you rip your boss's or senior manager's ideas in front of everyone, frequently point out what is wrong with what they are doing, or go out of your way to disagree with the person. Those things are politically stupid. We are saying that you don't waste any of your precious time and energy on the kissers except to note what not to do.

Poor Personal Hygiene

By this I mean that someone may smell bad; their clothes, shoes, fingernails, and/or hair are unclean; their breath is unbearable. There are three options to solving this problem.

Leave a note. Leave an unsigned note telling the person what's bothering you and how it is affecting you and your work and others and their work. Ask that the individual do something about it.

Drop a hint. For bad breath, leave Listerine Breath Strips or Tic Tacs on the office chair. For dirty fingernails, leave a list from the yellow pages of manicure shops, or leave an orange stick for cleaning nails or a picture of clean hands on the desk.

Tell it like it is. If you are bold and think you can handle it with the least hurt to the colleague's feelings, take the person aside. Come clean with the coworker about the problem and offer to help the individual.

Talking Too Loudly or Yelling

Colleagues who raise their voices or start yelling can really unnerve you. For example, the person may talk too loudly during staff meetings or a management retreat. It could happen when the person is making a point or disagreeing with you or someone else. Yelling can occur when you and he are having a one-on-one meeting to talk about a project or problem. Here are some suggestions to try.

Bring it down. Notch your voice down from your usual volume. Let the person talking too loudly know that it is difficult to comprehend what she is saying. Remain calm, cool, and composed. This works wonders because not only will your coworker have to concentrate to hear you, but decreasing your own voice volume is a cue to her to do the same.

Be direct. If lowering your own voice doesn't work, ask your coworker to lower his voice. Tell him that you want to keep things professional and remind the person that the conversation is between two cordial colleagues.

Take a time-out. If the coworker continues to talk loudly, let him know that you will need to leave right now and will be happy to take up the conversation again later when he has had a chance to calm down.

Lack of Follow-Up

If someone promises to deliver something to you by a certain time but doesn't, commits to helping you with a project or problem but doesn't mention it again, or says she'll call you to talk further about what you were discussing, but never gets back to you, that's lack of follow-up. Lack of follow-up could also mean promising to get you a certain price on a part or to make sure you get credit for your contribution on an exciting breakthrough for your company, but not making it happen. Here are some tried-and-true solutions.

Spell out the consequence. Let the person know right up front how what she is working on fits into what you are working on; present at least a quick glimpse of the whole picture. If she misses the deadline, let her know what impact it has on the end result. Find out why she missed the deadline and what you or she can do about it next time so it doesn't happen again.

Figure out how to help. If the problem is that your coworker consistently promises something and just never does anything after, try to decipher why this happens. Is it because he has so much on his plate and is forgetting? If this is the case, then have him write it down. Or perhaps you have to learn to follow up in an e-mail or a voice mail shortly after he's promised something. Reiterate in your reminder what he promised and when.

If your coworker agrees to do things because it's easier to say yes to you than to tell you no, then sit down, talk about what you both can do, and build some trust between the two of you.

Off-Color or Offensive Humor

Sometimes colleagues tell what they believe to be funny stories or jokes that you feel are completely out of line. Off-color or offensive humor may be a joke with sexual innuendo. It may be making fun of someone who is fat or skinny, old or young, gay or lesbian. Something offensive could also be a racially insensitive or religiously intolerant joke. Here are some suggestions.

Make your point directly and briefly. Tell your coworker that what she has just said is not funny to you. Say that you would appreciate that she not make those kinds of comments or jokes around you.

Don't be defensive. Don't belabor your point by giving an explanation about why it is offensive or unappealing to you.

Tell HR. If the colleague's comments are of a sexual nature or tone, try to handle it yourself the first time it happens. If it occurs again, talk with HR. Employers usually have a zero-tolerance policy on sexual harassment, which includes not being subjected to a "hostile" working environment—one in which you feel under attack or diminished. You will be doing your colleagues a favor by stopping this unacceptable behavior as quickly as you can.

Managing a New Group

HAVE YOU JUST BEEN PROMOTED and are you inheriting a new staff? Will you be managing for the first time? Or have you held many managerial positions but still have some jitters about taking on the big responsibility of a new team? Have you been handed the challenge of a low-morale or underperforming group of employees because of your excellent management skills?

● DEFINING THE CHALLENGE

Managing a new group can be problematic for many reasons. There could be performance issues that the previous manager did not deal with. You could be walking into a situation of low morale, high turnover and absenteeism, and low productivity. Competition and infighting might be hampering the group's performance and cohesiveness. Key openings that have gone unfilled for a long time may be dragging the group down because everyone is overworked and on edge. The team may be ready for mutiny owing to a perceived lack of career development or recognition, or what the members consider to be the inappropriate pay. The staff could be suffering from a previous void in leadership or direction. People could be angry or unclear about changes in the organization that impacted them (new reporting relationships, budget cuts, a hiring freeze, higher performance expectations).

The group could also be resistant to change. Maybe its members don't like change or perhaps they have tried it in the past and it either failed or they got burned—felt harmed in some way. Your new employees could be immature with a serious entitlement attitude: You owe them what they want, what they feel they deserve. Lastly, you could be managing a new group that is burned out, pure and simple. Maybe employees have been working extreme hours or have made it through a crisis or an extensive project for the organization. They are tired and stressed.

● Facing the Challenge

Managing people is a challenge unto itself that takes constant effort, like any relationship or partnership. When stepping into a new group, you'll find it's like starting from scratch all over again. You have to build each individual relationship. You need to gain the trust and respect of your new employees. You need to provide direction, leadership, coaching, and development to your people and still do your own work all at the same time.

Becoming a great manager requires a variety of aspirations, attitudes, and actions. From my experience advising and developing managers, there are seven attributes that can make an ordinary manager extraordinary. They tend to do or embrace what I call the seven C's (see Figure 9-1).

Model the Core Values and Culture

The enduring adage is to lead by example. Actions do indeed speak volumes. Don't just espouse the organization's values and culture, live them, lead the charge, model them in everything you say and do. This means, for example, that if you say that respect for others is a company value, then you show your respect for others in your everyday dealings with your staff, your colleagues, and outsiders. If part of the company culture is supposed to be admitting mistakes and taking responsibility to fix them, then if you make a mistake, you will handle it without pointing fingers.

Connect with Your Employees

Make a point of knowing each of the people who report to you. Treat them as individuals, valued both singly and as a group. Meet with each of them individually, even if your schedule is extremely busy. Setting aside 30 minutes for each person over a few weeks or stretched over a few months is a smart investment in your people. It will show you are making the effort

Figure 9-1. The Seven C's of Becoming a Great Manager

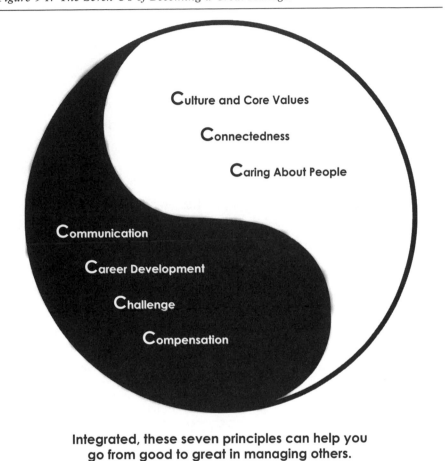

Culture and Core Values

Connectedness

Caring About People

Communication

Career Development

Challenge

Compensation

**Integrated, these seven principles can help you
go from good to great in managing others.**

to connect with them and get to know them as people, not parts in your machinery.

When you meet with each of your direct reports, find out about his or her background, experience, what he or she does, and what's on his or her mind. Ask:

- What are your key challenges, priorities, or missed opportunities during the past year?
- How do you define success for yourself and your staff?
- What do you want?

- What motivates and inspires you?
- If you had three things you could wish for from me, what would they be?

If your direct reports have their own staff, you want to get to know about these people as well. Spend at least the last 20 minutes of your time asking them to give an overview of each person who reports to them. Ask them to share with you their backgrounds, problems, what they do, and potential for advancing.

Ask Human Resources to pull the employee files on each of your new staff members and also for their people. Review the files to gain a sense of performance reviews, backgrounds, special recognitions, specific skills, and problems. If there are employee surveys or "climate" surveys that have been used in the past to measure areas like employee job satisfaction or morale, ask for those reports so that you can get a quick overview of what kind of a situation you are inheriting.

One word of caution: Even if your company embraces a hierarchical organizational culture, do your best not to reproduce that culture within your own group. Instead, try to consider the people with whom you work as team members or as valued partners. You can usually coexist peacefully with the more hierarchical managers in your organization while creating something different for your own team. Your people will appreciate this approach.

Communicate Clearly and Often

Use a variety of ways to communicate with your staff:

- *In person.* Use town hall–style meetings with the group, one-on-one touch-base meetings with individuals.
- *Electronically.* Send e-mail selectively; pass along important information quickly while you are out of the office; point your team to links or Web sites that they can review more leisurely.
- *In writing.* In this age of high technology, a personal touch is a gesture that makes a big impression. Send a handwritten note or a

thanks or compliment scribbled on a report, press clipping, or customer letter.

The above is the "how" of communicating. The "what" is multifaceted as well. Put yourself in your staff's shoes. What would you want to hear about if you were in their place? Usually employees are eager to learn about the following:

- How the company is doing; how it compares to competitors; overall industry trends and themes on the horizon
- Any changes (small shifts to larger turnabouts) in direction, strategy, or priorities
- When someone important to their existence and work is coming, leaving, or doing something that will impact them
- How the group's priorities, goals, and objectives fit into the company's as a whole
- How the group is doing
- Individual contributions that have helped elevate the overall performance of the team
- What's on your mind and what's on your plate

Make It Okay to Challenge

Create an environment where it's safe and even encouraged for your employees to challenge you and each other. Consider what things would be like if everyone always agreed with each other or if all of your team said yes to everything you thought or said. You'd be redundant! Your team would suffer group-think and lose the diversity of ideas, opinions, and perspectives that are vital to achieving the best outcomes. But making it okay for employees to challenge does not mean that it's all right to do it disrespectfully or as an attack. Teach your team how to challenge and be challenged effectively and in a way that strengthens rather than divides the group.

Coach and Support Career Development

Even if your own manager is not supportive of your career or development, don't pass that lack of direction on to your employees. Coach them by giving them constructive feedback, using facts to specifically identify the problems or approaches for how they could have done better. Work together to come up with the solutions. Support your people to achieve success. Proactively provide career development by having regular discussions about what interests them, helping them figure out what the next move might be and how to get there, recognizing any skill gaps they need to work on, and so on.

Ideally you want each of your staff to be the best that he or she can become. If one of them becomes your boss or maybe even the CEO, you have done a great job! Truly, your objective is that they move on to bigger and better things. That's the ultimate gift you can give your company. On Maslow's Hierarchy of Needs, the highest level one can ascend to is transcendence—using what gifts and experience you have to help others reach their highest potential.

Compensate with Tangibles *and* Intangibles

People are not motivated only by money. Total compensation in the broadest sense is the sum total of everything that the employee receives that is of value to him or to her from you, the company, the job, the environment, colleagues, and so on. Use the tools, levers, and incentives that most motivate and reward your people. These include:

> Base pay, stock options, bonuses
> Financial support for career development programs
> Flexible schedules or job sharing
> Sabbaticals or time off
> Changes to job responsibilities
> Better titles
> Old-fashioned praise and recognition for a job well done
> Fun events or celebrations together for letting off steam, team building, or as a reward

Care About People

This may sound harsh, but if you don't care about people you should not accept management responsibility. Managing others is not for everyone and it does not have to be the only way you can get a promotion, more pay, responsibility, or power if those are important to you. In the companies I worked in, for example, we created both technical and managerial tracks. This meant that someone who was technically excellent in the job who either did not want to manage others or who was not effective at it could move up (bigger job, better pay and title, etc.) yet continue not to manage a staff.

Caring about people means that you will use your heart as well as your mind when making managerial decisions. You will be sensitive to the fact that the person you are dealing with is a human being with feelings, emotions, vulnerabilities, and a personal life outside of work. You can still be professional and do what is best for the business, but you will factor the people side into your decision. For example, if someone has been a stellar performer and has recently hit some emotionally difficult times (death in the family, alcoholism or drug addiction, divorce, etc.), you may indeed make an exception to the general rules for that employee. Maybe he can work from home one day a week. Perhaps you will give him extra time for a deadline. It could be that you take some extra time with the person to give him more guidance than usual.

Caring about people also means that you make the effort to look beneath the surface. Granted, you are probably stretched pretty thin with not enough hours in your day. Being a great manager means sensing the vibes and feeling the pulse of the people who work with you. No matter how much you make it conducive for your people to tell you things, some are not genetically coded that way. It's your job not to pull teeth but, rather, to know your individual team members well enough that you can know when something is out of kilter and take the initiative to discuss it.

● RECOMMENDED RESOURCES

Managing people at its best becomes leadership. I asked one of the best leaders or managers I know to give his top picks on books that have inspired and developed him throughout his extraordinary career in industry and academia. William F. Meehan III, Director of McKinsey and Company; Senior Lecturer in Strategic Management and Class of 1978 Lecturer, 2004-2005, for the Stanford University Graduate School of Business, shares his recommendations and insights. These eclectic books are valuable in providing foundation, core concepts, innovative ideas, and inspiration for what it takes to be a great manager and leader.

Meehan's List

1. *On Leadership* by John Gardner. "For the business leader who wants to understand leadership deeply."

2. *Good to Great* by Jim Collins. "A book about how management and leadership can elevate an organization from good to great from the best of our current business gurus."

3. *The Art of War* by Sun Tzu. "Business isn't war but many of the principles apply."

4. Winston Churchill. "Any biography about the archetypal Western leader of the 20th century gives insights into influencing and leading people."

5. *The Will to Manage* by Marvin Bower. "Principle-centered business leadership in one of its earliest forms."

6. *The Consolations of Philosophy* by Alain de Botton. "For the leader who is more a thinker than a list maker."

7. *The 7 Habits of Highly Effective People* by Stephen Covey. "Every leader faces a Sunday night when they need to change. This is the book to start with."

8. *The Prince* by Niccolo Machiavelli. "Still the foundation text on the political nuances of leadership."

9. *Soul of a New Machine* by Tracy Kidder. "The best book about innovation."

10. *In Search of Excellence* by Tom Peters and Bob Waterman. "Valuable insights about what makes organizations and the people in them excellent."

11. *Competitive Strategy* by Michael Porter. "The basic strategy text."

12. *The Borderless World* by Ken Ohmae. "From the last era of globalization but more relevant now than then."

13. *Creative Destruction* by Dick Foster. "The most fundamental book on what shapes business performance over long periods of time."

14. *Primer on Decision Making: How Decisions Happen* by James G. March. "A look at decision making as one that interprets action as rational choice."

15. *The Limits of Organization* (Fels Lectures on Public Policy Analysis) by Kenneth Joseph Arrow. "An interesting read. The book is based on a lecture series that explores public choice concepts with respect to organizations."

My Top Ten List

For those newer to managing others who are looking for how to's, here's my Top Ten list of books:

1. *Competitive Advantage Through People* by Jeffrey Pfeffer. An excellent book from one of my favorite professors at Stanford Business School discusses how to achieve performance through people.

2. *1001 Ways to Reward Employees* by Bob Nelson. Low-cost ideas and proven strategies to motivate and reward your employees.

3. *Kiss, Bow, or Shake Hands* by Terri Morrison, Wayne A. Conaway, and George A. Borden, Ph.D. An oldie but goodie on doing business cross-culturally. The principles can also apply to managing a culturally diverse workforce.

4. *Managing Transitions* by William Bridges. Helps us as managers understand how to make the most of change as well as guide others through it.

5. *Time Bind . . . When Work Becomes Home and Home Becomes Work* by Arlie Russell Hochschild. Gives an understanding of work and family challenges that employees and organizations are grappling with.

6. *Setting Global Standards* by S. Prakash Sethi. With the focus on ethics and social responsibility in organizations and their management, this book is a good foundation on creating codes of conduct in multinational corporations.

7. *Leading Quietly: An Unorthodox Guide to Doing the Right Thing* by Joseph L. Badaracco. This is a practical guide to resolving everyday leadership dilemmas.

8. *Words You Don't Want to Hear During Your Annual Review: A* Dilbert *Book* by Scott Adams. A comical but enlightening view of what not to do so that you're not the bad, evil, or idiot boss.

9. *Never Give In* edited by Winston S. Churchill. The best of Winston Churchill's speeches, edited by his grandson.

10. *The Tipping Point* by Malcolm Gladwell. How little things make a big difference.

Other Resources

• American Management Association Seminars–*http://www.amanet.org/index.htm.* Excellent free learning resources, information on seminars, and certificate program on a broad range of subjects, management and supervisory, leadership, communication skills, finance, marketing, and others.

• *Harvard Business Review* and Press–*http://www.harvardbusiness online.* A collection of the best management ideas. Books, articles, newsletters, the *Harvard Business Review* publication, interviews with executives, case studies, conferences, e-learning opportunities on topics ranging from getting the most out of your team members to how CEOs can manage growth agendas.

• Workforce Management–*http://www.workforce.com.* A valuable online resource for a wide range of tips on managing your workforce or employees. Search relevant categories: compensation and benefits, recruiting and staffing, training and development, and technology.

Asking for a Raise or Promotion

HAVE YOU BEEN WORKING like a dog but not gotten the raise that you deserve? Do you know what your friends and colleagues in similar jobs are making and there's a big disparity? Have you kept quiet for too long, keeping your head down and doing your work, but it's time to speak up about a raise? Did you and your friend both start in the company around the same time, but he has gotten several big raises and a promotion while you have not? Were you initially willing to join the company knowing you were overqualified and underpaid, with the expectation that you would catch up over time? Can you honestly say that your manager is taking credit for your work with the higher-ups who make the compensation decisions? Is your manager receiving the monetary rewards that you deserve at least part or all of?

Maybe you were promised when you joined the organization that you had lots of potential and headroom for your career to progress and were advised to be patient, but you have not seen anything happen yet. Have you been passed over for a promotion a few times now with people hired in from outside or even from inside the company—people you believe are less qualified than you are? Have you delivered breathtaking results for the company and delivered time and again, but you are not being paid fairly what you are worth?

● DEFINING THE CHALLENGE

Asking for a raise or a promotion can be scary. Most often people fear rejection or, worse yet, that somehow asking will be a CLM (career-limiting move). If you are going to ask for a raise or promotion, you have to deserve it and know your worth—your true value to your employer. At the extreme, you may have to be willing to walk out the door to find a job that will pay you what is fair market value for what you do or to have a shot at the promotion you want so badly.

● FACING THE CHALLENGE

If you are sure you deserve a raise or a promotion, you should have no qualms about asking for it. However, getting a raise or promotion is all about *your* contributions to the organization. You must talk about what you bring to the table, not speak negatively about your fellow employees. Whatever you do, don't wing it when you meet with your boss. Get your facts together, the ones that prove your value to the department and to the company as a whole. This chapter will offer strategies and tips, including talking points, for asking for a raise and going for a promotion.

Asking for a Raise

Know your market value. Do your homework to understand what you are truly worth in today's market. This may prove to be a rude awakening— perhaps you are even overpaid. It could also be an eye-opener if you find that you are woefully underpaid, especially for your experience and background. To find your market value:

- Talk with some executive recruiter friends or contacts and find out what employers are paying for people with your background and scope of job responsibilities.
- Selectively search on a few key Web sites and see what job descriptions similar to yours are paying. (See the end of this chapter and Chapter 1, where there are a variety of Web sites to draw from.)
- Ask around to your colleagues in similar organizations and get them to give you a salary range for what they are paid.
- If you are in a professional association or meet regularly with a group of colleagues, ask everyone to share confidentially to the group his compensation. If yours is not competitive, use this infor-

mation as ammunition to build a strong case for asking for a well-deserved raise.

No "show me the money" attitude. Leave any attitude at the door. No one is entitled to more money. Although the job market is showing signs of recovery, it's still a buyer's (employer's) market owing to the oversupply of talented candidates and qualified people competing for jobs. If you want a raise, think about whether you deserve it. Have you earned it? If your answer is a resounding yes, think about some of the bigger considerations:

- Are budgets robust or being cut deeply?
- How is your organization performing overall?
- Has it had an excellent year of strong earnings or is it limping along in need of resuscitation?
- What is the compensation philosophy in your company? This means, what is the management perspective on how to pay and reward its employees:
  - Does your company choose to be in the upper 10 percent of the market with competitors and benchmark jobs, thus paying really well?
  - Does your company tend to pay on the low side because it offers so many other benefits, perks, and intangibles?

Reflecting on these sorts of questions will help you ascertain how your manager will receive your request and what realistically are the chances she can work to improve your compensation.

Develop a compelling, rational case. If you know in advance the objections or obstacles to your request that you could face, then use these as a base for developing a compelling case as to why you have earned and deserve a raise. Put together some talking points. Make sure to stop talking frequently and listen to what your manager has to say. (See the end of this chapter for some sample talking points.)

Think outside the box. Be ready to offer some creative ideas that are acceptable or desirable to you about how you can improve your compensation. Expand your definition of compensation. Compensation means more than annual salary and a bonus. Hear your manager's creative solutions. Be ready to suggest some of your own. (Some of my favorites are included in the talking points in the last section of this chapter.)

Practice your talking points. Speak your talking points out loud so you feel more comfortable when you are meeting with your manager. Ask a friend to rehearse with you and act as your boss may react. For example, if your boss will interrupt you, or scowl, or nod a lot but not really say anything, or try to put you off, have your friend do the same thing. Think about and practice how you would deal with each of those scenarios to keep things on track.

Find a conducive time to talk. Formally schedule a half-hour or hour with your manager. Avoid times when you know he will be extra rushed or stressed. Stay away from the few days right after he returns from an extended business trip. Try to go for a time and place that will enable quality time, but don't be put off. Be assertive about getting time on the calendar. Remember that you are important!

Be ready to walk out the door if you need to. Be smart and line up a job offer or two before you quit, if you can. Remember that your reputation is priceless, so handle your situation with class and grace. For example, you should not accept another job offer only as bait to get your current employer to pay you more.

If you think there's any chance your manager will try to get you to stay by offering you more money, but not until she is faced with the reality of losing you, then don't actually accept another offer when you receive it. Be honest; tell the new company that you are excited to receive the offer, but need some time to evaluate it since making a move is a big decision. Then speak with your manager as soon as possible, telling her about your job offer. If your company or manager makes you a counteroffer to keep you from leaving, think long and hard about whether you will stay. If you are going to decline the other company's offer, then do it as quickly and kindly as you can.

There's no easy way to let the other employer down, but some ways you can make the situation better are to refer a few qualified colleagues; do some consulting or project work on the side if it's not a conflict of interest with your current job; or promise to keep in touch and say you would consider working for them in the future—that the timing is not right now because you realize you still have things you want to accomplish in your current job.

Getting a Promotion

Master your current job. You'll need to consistently far exceed your performance goals and objectives and have a solid track record of valuable contributions to your team and organization before you can be considered for a promotion. Discuss the next steps in your career and your hopes with your manager, with Human Resources, with a mentor. Learn what experiences you need to have to be able to make the next move in your career.

Make your own luck. Keep your eyes open for promotional opportunities within your organization. Remember that ultimately you are the driver of your own career. If there is an opportunity for advancement, go through your company's formal process, such as turning in an application and a résumé, interviewing with the manager and other key people, and so on. You can also go the extra mile informally as long you do it within what is acceptable in your company's culture. For example, perhaps you ask your manager to be an advocate for you and speak with the other manager. You might ask your mentor to convey her support and your strengths to the hiring manager.

What if you think your manager will try to block your move? In that case, you will have to finesse your way to extricate yourself. That means you may have to talk with the hiring manager and let him know that you'd love to work with him but don't expect the support of your manager. If you are a great performer who is well respected, the hiring manager might go to bat for you. At minimum, he will be able to help your cause.

Show some chutzpah. If there's a job opening that would be a promotion for you, then ask for it outright. Like the jockey Red Pollard said in the film *Seabiscuit,* "There's my opening, I've got to go for it." If you've been in the organization for a while and are highly regarded, ask someone to give you a shot at the promotional opportunity.

Management may realize it's a stretch for you. There will probably be things you will need to learn and some gaps in your background or experience. Sometimes it is willing to overlook these shortcomings and support your career growth with reasonable risks. For example, realistically you could not move into a job that was critical to the company's success if you did not have all the qualifications or background to perform the full job well. However, you would be able to take on a job where there is a strong, seasoned team or manager around you to support you while you get up to speed or in which there are others doing the same job you would be doing so that they can pick up some of your slack for a while.

Try a career-broadening move. A promotion does not have to mean that you move the next step up the ladder. The traditional pyramid-structured career progression is antiquated. Today keeping a career moving and developing looks like a big spiral. Sometimes you move sideways, other times upward, sometimes even downward. There may even be times when you make a loop, coming back full circle.

Career broadening means that rather than trying to move up—to the next highest level—you move out, to a comparable job in another department. You choose a job that is similar in level to the one you have now but in a different function with different responsibilities. Career broadening is positive because you gain important experience in a wider range of jobs and functions. A broader base to draw from can strengthen a career down the road. Many career experts advise people to be generalists early in their careers, gaining as many varied experiences as they can. Later on, people can specialize and become the experts.

Offer to do a test drive. If you are set on a promotion, identify the people who are in those jobs. Cross-train with a colleague or two in the role you are hoping to assume. This can be done formally if your manager will support it. It can also be done informally. You can enlist help from your colleagues and they can teach you what they know. You can learn key parts of their jobs and even offer to fill in or help out with overflow work. Suggest that you try out the next job up the ladder and see how you do.

The caveat here is that in order for your colleagues to be willing to teach you, they must feel secure in their jobs and know that you will not attempt to push them out. Ideally, you will be going for an open position similar to those of your colleagues, but perhaps in a different division or group. Another ideal situation would be when you are privy to your colleague's plans to leave sometime in the short term. Maybe she is getting married and moving away, planning to take time off to start a family, or has been interviewing for other jobs.

Transfer out. Sometimes it's not possible to be promoted within your department or group; you need to make a move to elsewhere within your organization where there are promotional opportunities. Ask for your manager's support in doing this. Request that he champion your cause actively.

Persevere and keep on trying. You need only find a crack in the door or an open window—a manager who will take a chance on you and give you a shot at a promotion. For example, there was a woman I'll call Emma. She had a degree from a top school but had been toiling away for years as a receptionist. She was completely underutilized and tried for many other jobs within her organization. This was to no avail. She was about to give up and leave the company but decided one more time to interview for a job with a star manager who had just been given a big promotion and lots more responsibility herself. This manager needed to quickly fill eight openings that had gone unfilled for over a year, as well as to bring in key talent for roles she had created for her new group.

Coaching the manager about building a stronger-performing, high-morale team, I encouraged her to take a chance on Emma, hiring her to an exempt job many levels above where she had been for so long. This ended up as a win-win situation with great results. Emma was so appreciative to have the chance; she was a dedicated, above-the-call-of-duty employee who was also loyal to her manager. Performance-wise, Emma delivered in all areas of her responsibilities. At last check, the manager decided to make a wonderful career change, leaving the company herself. She recommended that Emma succeed her, and she did.

Jump ship. If you are convinced you deserve a promotion (or a raise) and you have tried everything you can with no result, then start looking for another job—discreetly. You may need to leave your employer. Keep in mind, however, that this is risky and has its own set of potential drawbacks, such as having to build back up a track record of performance, establish new relationships, and so on.

● TOOLS AND RESOURCES

Web Sites for Finding Out What You're Worth
- Bureau of Labor Statistics—*www.bls.gov*. Review statistics, news, "Economy at a Glance," "Occupational Handbook."
- JobStar—*http://jobstar.org/tools/salary/index.htm*. Salary information by industry, job function, location. Links to *Wall Street Journal*.
- CareerJournal.com—*www.careerjournal.com*. Articles on salaries and options.
- Salary.com—*www.salary.com*. Use the salary wizard tool, articles, job postings, and career resources.
- Wage Web—*www.wageweb.com*. Site includes over 150 benchmark positions and compensation data for each.
- For mid-career to executive level jobs, take a look at Chapter 1 on doing a job search.

Review the Web sites on executive recruiters in Chapter 1. If you can network into one of them, they could provide a quick and valuable take on the market and value for your background.

Sample Talking Points to Ask for a Raise

Here are some suggestions for approaching your boss about that raise:

- "Thank you for taking the time to meet with me. I have something important to both of us that I would like to discuss and get your input on."
- "When I joined the company and your group, I was willing to take a cut in pay because of the excitement I had about working with you and the amount of valuable contribution I knew I could make. You told me there was lots of headroom and potential for a salary in-

crease and I'd like to discuss that today. It's been close to eleven months now."

- "Here's why I believe I deserve a raise: I completed the *xyz* project under budget and ahead of time. The new product launch is already producing revenues beyond our expectations. You have probably seen the last statistics I provided you [highlight quantifiable results here]."

Briefly state a few points about why you deserve the raise. Examples are:

- How much money you have saved the company through X
- How you have increased market share in a specific region
- How you have improved revenues or profit
- How you have turned around a bad situation, such as high employee turnover or a litigious staff that was ready to file a class action lawsuit
- How you saved some key managers who were ready to walk out the door
- How you have developed two people on your team who are ready to take on key roles within the organization—positions you normally would have had to fill with hires from the outside and pay 30 to 40 percent executive recruiter fees on their first-year annual compensation
- How you have improved the reputation of the company or cleaned up a potentially explosive scandal
- How you came up with a winning new product idea or a break-through of some sort for the company
- What your specific contributions to a bigger overall project were

If you are asking for a raise around the time that merit increases are being decided and you believe you deserve a much bigger "bump" in pay than the average, here are some sample talking points:

- "I've read the HR materials about the merit increase budgets and know that the average is expected to come in at 5 percent."

- "I believe I warrant a much bigger increase than that. If it can't be done during the annual merit increase timing, we could think about some creative ways to increase my total compensation with some other components or do another increase six months after this one coming up."

Creative Compensation Components

Here are some other ways to realize greater compensation on the job:

- A bump up to the next grade or level in my job category.
- A better title (this can help you get a better job at some point when you do decide to leave the company; for example, you could be given the working title of "manager" or become an "executive director," up from a "director." Perhaps you are named a group manager, project lead, operations specialist, department leader, or a senior "something," such as senior writer, senior inventory analyst, or senior buyer.
- A spot bonus. Try for a one-time bonus for extraordinary work on a particular project, contribution to the group or company, and so on.
- Extra stock options.
- Mid-year merit increase (if merit increases are given annually, you may be granted one at six months as well).
- A few extra weeks of vacation time.
- A trip to a great location for a conference, or training program, to give a talk, or to recruit for the organization.
- Financial support toward your career development, such as tuition for a specific executive education program or a course that will enhance your job performance.
- Something of value for your partner, spouse, or child. For example, your spouse can use the company's career center for her job search; free child care at the child care center for your child; your partner considered for a contract or project with the company, as long as it is transparent and awarded within company policy.

Feeling Inadequate at Your Job

HAVE YOU MOVED UP the company ladder at a good pace, but find yourself less sure of your competence on the latest rung you've reached? Is it getting harder and harder to maintain the confidence to master the job and perform to your own and others' high expectations? Are you in a role in which you are out of your league, without the experience or know-how to adequately handle parts of the job? Have you recently been promoted but don't feel like you have gotten up to speed yet? Have you taken on a much larger scope of responsibilities and staff, but deep down you don't feel that you know what you are doing? Do you feel inadequate, like you are falling short, or that somehow you'll be found out as an imposter, not the high performer people think you are?

● DEFINING THE CHALLENGE

If any of these scenarios sounds familiar to you, you may have reached a career plateau that many people define as "The Peter Principle." This is an old theory that says people rise to their highest level of incompetence. In other words, someone keeps getting promoted and promoted because of proven competence at the job until he or she reaches a point at which he or she is actually incompetent—unable to perform effectively. As our British friends would say, this is pure hogwash.

Based on my experiences developing executives and high-potential managers, and establishing company succession plans, I don't believe in the

Peter Principle. I do believe that you can be incompetent in some aspects of your job, especially as you move into new positions with a greater scope of responsibilities. However, how you overcome that incompetence is what matters to your future success on the job.

● FACING THE CHALLENGE

Incompetence in some areas of your skills, knowledge, or abilities can used as an impetus to change, learn, develop, and grow. Incompetence can be embraced as something you have just not learned or mastered yet. We are capable of learning most anything if we set our minds to it. If you put out the effort, you can transform your incompetence into an eventual capability. If something truly is impossible for you to master or there's just not enough time for acquiring a new capability, you can always tap into the knowledge and skills of others. That's why very capable, accomplished, and successful people build strong teams around them or occasionally bring in a pinch hitter to handle a specific task. There are people you can bring in to do the work that you cannot do. This doesn't make you a failure. It makes you human and an accessible leader or manager who is self-aware of areas on which you need help.

Here are some lessons learned. These will help you overcome the Peter Principle if you think you have reached it.

Break Out of Your Comfort Zone

Accept that you're only human. Having certain areas that you are not so great in makes you human. It's not possible to come into a new situation, a new project, or a new company or group or start to learn a new business or function and master all the details immediately. When you're trying to accomplish something right off the bat in an area where you have little experience, it's only natural that you feel like you don't know what you are doing. Most people can connect with and relate to this feeling. Your acceptance of this inadequacy makes you more real to others, especially people you supervise. If you're not uptight or freaking out about not being able to perform some aspect of your responsibilities immediately, then others won't be uptight or freak out, either.

Accept that there will be areas of incompetence any time you take on a new challenge, especially something as enormous as a higher-level job with new responsibilities. You may feel like there is an overwhelming amount to learn, be it a new area of the business, the new landscape of people and players, or how to call up skills that either you don't have or that you have considered weaknesses. Be aware of what knowledge you don't have a handle on. Get the help or expertise that you need. Use the following tips to turn incompetence into a new capability.

Follow a fresh take on the 80-20 rule. You have probably heard of the 80-20 rule. It is a well-known principle in sales and related fields, for example, that 80 percent of your revenues are the result of 20 percent of your customers. Variations on the rule abound, but the basic idea is that 80 percent of your successful results come from 20 percent of your efforts.

In a career context, the 80-20 rule can be used to keep careers thriving. Those who practice it stay stimulated, productive, and willing to take healthy risks in the roles they accept or choose. My fresh take on the 80-20 rule gives you a successful way to keep growing and developing in your career. To accomplish this, you want to take on roles that 80 percent of the time allow you to draw on strengths, prior experience, and core skills. The other 20 percent of your efforts should take you out of your comfort zone. They should be a stretch for you. This means taking on challenges and trying your hand at responsibilities, activities, and skills that are not part of your normal experience. These challenges will have a steep learning curve. Attempting them may make you feel incompetent. But putting out the effort to get better or actually master them will add to your repertoire of capabilities and give you a strong sense of achievement.

The point is that it's okay and even desired to feel incompetent for a while, but you should never feel incapable. You will take steps to acquire the new knowledge, build the necessary skills, or do whatever is needed to either master the 20 percent or make sure it gets handled by someone else who is capable.

Embrace your learning curve. In any new project, activity, or skill, there's an initial phase in which you are not efficient or productive. As you gain in knowledge or experience, you become more efficient and productive exponentially, finally reaching a peak or a high point. This is the basis of a learning curve.

For example, you may have strengths and experience in working at an entertainment company. Then you join a technology-related company and have to learn the business and operations from scratch. How do you most quickly and effectively do that? You can identify key people and ask them to tell you everything they think you should know. You can read some valuable books on the field, take a crash course or program, hire a coach, or just learn by diving in and using trial and error (if you can afford to). The idea is to figure out what you need to know and start the learning process right away. Fully embrace your learning curve; don't shy away from it.

Accept that "Best All Around" is good enough. You can't score a perfect 10 in every single aspect of your role or job. You cannot perform each responsibility with perfect skill and mastery. No one expects this of you. What you do want is to handle the majority of what you do exceptionally well. The other 10 percent or so can be okay or good, not great. Everything cannot be your strong suit, so accept that you can be the best all around.

Stretch Yourself

Keep working to improve. Developing your capabilities, skills, and competencies is an ongoing effort. Even when you are more experienced in your career, you need to keep at it. (Take a look at Chapter 12 on career development.)

Here's a way to design your own career development plan:

1. Make a list of the 10 strengths and competencies you think you will need to have the ultimate career you want.

2. Identify which of these you don't have now that you can start working on.

3. Prioritize them and selectively use your time to cultivate each of them.

For example, maybe you recognize that you need to learn how to hire and fire people, deal with change or chaos, or develop your financial management skills. What do you need to do? What are the resources you can utilize? What can you start doing now so that you can develop these over time?

Seek out jobs that will stretch you. Most people play to their strengths. There are some career experts who will say to forget about areas that you are weak in and to keep leveraging your strengths. There is a lot to be said about that approach. For some people, that works and having a career built around that premise is highly gratifying. Every so often, there's nothing wrong with taking a job that you "could do in your sleep" and in which you can soar from day one. However, I regularly encourage people to seek jobs that will stretch them. Over a lifetime, the jobs that require you to take on roles and responsibilities that are outside your comfort zone and that stretch you to the maximum are the ones where you learn the most and gain confidence for the next challenge.

Build a Strong Team

Hire people who are smarter than you are. If you know you have some gaps in your knowledge or some competencies that are weak, hire people who complement you. Hire people who are smarter and better than you in the dimensions you are lacking.

If you have made your mark as a marketing whiz but don't know much about accounting, be sure you hire or promote someone who is an expert in that area. This doesn't mean that you should abdicate all responsibilities in these areas. You still need to understand what's needed and why, determine how each competency fits into the big picture, and add some overall value in these areas. You don't have to be the one to do them masterfully, however.

Look for people who complement your abilities. There may be times when you are promoted and do not have the luxury of time to learn something that is critical. This is especially true if you manage a large group of people. If there is someone in the organization or on the outside who can do this specific task better than you can, bring him in. In the bigger picture, such a complementary player can be a valuable addition to the team. And it can mean the difference between winning or losing.

For example, maybe you were just promoted to be head of a new international division. You are known and respected for your innovative ideas but are somewhat weaker in implementation. You would be wise to hire a strong Number Two person, kind of a second-in-command, who is incredible at execution. Together, the two of you can accomplish a whole lot more and do it much faster.

Bring in a pinch hitter. Suppose you are a very rational, measured, unemotional leader, but your team now needs an infusion of passion, creativity, or more free-flowing energy. Rather than morph into something you are not and come off as not authentic, bring in what you need through someone who can pinch hit for you.

For example, let someone in HR play that role, someone who really understands the business and who is respected by your group. Encourage one of your up-and-coming managers, or a possible successor, to provide what you need to the group. You can bring the pinch hitter into key strategy or planning sessions. He or she can attend your staff meetings. Maybe you call on the person episodically when you need a quick, strong dose to provide what you cannot.

● TOOLS AND RESOURCES

Filling the Competency Gaps

Figure 11-1 is a worksheet for noting your strengths, comparing them to the qualifications for a new job, and determining what competencies you are missing—where you have gaps. Use this worksheet to identify your key gaps and to begin to map out how to fill in those gaps to become closer to fulfilling all that your new job requires.

- List your current strengths that you can utilize in your new job.
- List the competencies and strengths required in your new job—the one in which you fear reaching the Peter Principle.

Figure 11-1. Find the Gap

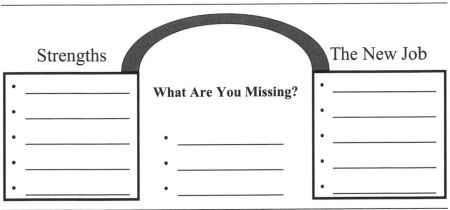

- Note which competencies and strengths you are missing. What are your gaps?
- How will you deal with each of the gaps? At least one gap should be a stretch goal for you. Figure out what steps you can take and what resources you need to develop the competence quickly.
- For the other gaps, determine if there is time for you to develop the competency as you go along. How will you do this?
- If you have to bring in someone else with the competence to immediately fill the need, how can you do this most effectively? Is there someone on your team you can promote, then rehire for her position? Or will you have to call on expertise from outside your group, such as someone from elsewhere in the company or from outside?

Having No Career Path

ARE YOU STUCK in a dead-end job? Do you have trouble seeing how you can advance within your company? Have you watched others in your organization get promoted time and again, but you're becoming frustrated because you can't seem to get anywhere? Perhaps you have a wide range of interests but are unclear about what different opportunities there are in your organization. Is your manager too ambitious with his own career to help you with yours? Perhaps he is nice enough but just does not have the know-how or time to invest in your professional development. Maybe career development is not a high priority for your company. Does it seem like your organization is woefully lacking in resources, initiatives, and programs for the development of its employees?

● DEFINING THE CHALLENGE

Do any of these scenarios strike a chord with you? This is what having no (or little) career path or development looks like. Basically it's when you want to develop your career and grow professionally, but this ambition is not supported by either your manager or your company. This is a problem because if the situation goes on indefinitely you will feel powerless. You can lose motivation, become resentful, or turn unproductive. Plus, it's just not enjoyable and not stimulating to be in a job that you think is going nowhere.

● FACING THE CHALLENGE

You are ultimately the boss of your own career. There are some companies that don't seem to encourage career development among their employees, even some that may seem to stifle it, but there's no point in complaining or pointing fingers. This chapter will focus on how to take charge of your own career path and development. We will discuss how to create your own path as well as leverage any and all resources inside or outside your organization.

Own Your Career

Decide on your focus. At this point, are you interested in career broadening or career advancement? There is a big difference and each can be an important part of your career path and development.

Career broadening means learning a variety of skills and competencies as you determine where your future lies. Working in different jobs in a variety of functional areas and departments allows you to test-drive jobs and try different groups on for size. Then you can determine which job or group you want to focus on. Career broadening serves as a strong foundation for moving up over time. Your base of strengths, experience in the company, knowledge of the various areas within the company, and relationships you will have established are a potent combination. On the other hand, career advancing means moving up on a natural or defined career ladder. For example, in a consulting firm, someone may progress through the roles of associate/analyst, engagement manager, senior engagement manager, and, eventually, principal.

In some industries and at some companies, the career-advancement path is easy to recognize. You have to follow it if you want your career to develop.

Take the initiative with your manager. Schedule a time to meet with your manager. Try for a time that is most conducive for listening and engaging, when there's a lull in the work or a few days after your boss has returned from vacation or a trip. Explain that you realize how busy she is and appreciate the time.

Express to your manager that your career is very important to you. You truly need and would appreciate the manager's advice and coaching. Be clear on your objectives. For example, you'd like to brainstorm about possible next career moves, what more you need to accomplish in your current position, and what you can be doing in your current job to keep developing. Try to come away from the discussion with two or three concrete career development objectives for the year. For example, they could be something like:

- Take a Webinar (seminar on the Web) in X topic.
- Volunteer for a company-wide task force related to X topic.
- Meet with managers in X group and HR to discuss potential next moves or jobs in X area.

Develop yourself. You may have to go it alone—do your career development without the support of your manager. If you have tried to enlist her help and it's just not working, realize it's not worth your efforts. Although this is not an ideal situation, at some point it becomes futile to keep trying to convince the manager to offer active involvement. As long as your manager is not an obstacle to what you are trying to achieve, you should be okay. It is hoped there will be other people or resources in your organization that you can call on.

Don't let a bad manager throw you off course. There are managers out there who are insecure in their jobs and see their employees as competition or don't want to be outperformed by their own direct reports. In some unfortunate cases, they actually try to sabotage their employees' efforts. There is nothing within your control to do about this, so just do what you can do. Perform well. Develop a track record, making sure higher-ups and others are aware of what you contribute. Cultivate relationships with other managers or their employees whose opinions count. Try to get out from under your manager as quickly as you can. Life is too short to work with this kind of manager. Find somewhere else in the organization with a better manager.

You don't want to bad-mouth your manager. The common wisdom is that if you do that to the manager, you'll do that to others, too. Most people usually know the managers who don't develop or do worse things to their employees. It serves no purpose for you to spend the energy to let people know about what your manager is doing or not doing for you.

Gain Your Company's Support

Research programs and courses available to you. These could be community college courses, professional conferences or seminars for your industry or the particular field you are in or wish to move into, workshops, or online programs.

Good sources of information include:

- American Management Association—*www.amanet.org/.* American Management Association International is the world's largest membership-based training organization. These experts offer training, business seminars, and professional development in a broad range of areas.
- Career Architect—*www.lominger.com.* This is something that we used in industry for developing high-potential employees in their careers. It is a career management and development tool that defines 67 leadership competencies along with a series of career starters and stoppers that allow you to measure your own capacity for executive leadership and to design your own development plan.
- Noontime University, Inc.—*www.noontimeu.com.* This group offers a wide variety of interactive on-site courses and teleclasses, often during the lunch hour. These developmental opportunities for busy professionals range from programs and certification courses on Adobe Illustrator, to primers on leadership skills, development of a strategic plan, financial management for nonfinancial managers, advanced project management skills, and tips on building teams and customer service.

Ask for company financial support. See if the company will pay for some part or all of the costs of a program or course that you choose. If the course or program is relevant to your current job, often the company will be willing. State the case about why the extra learning or skills building will improve your performance. Offer to write a formal report about what you learned or how the program benefits your work.

Find out how jobs are filled. Where are the job openings for your organization posted? Is there a Web site, a binder of jobs, a listing in your employee newsletter? Perhaps there is no formal process. If that's the case, you have to make sure you find out how to get into the flow of information.

Tap into the grapevine. If jobs are often filled before anyone really knows they exist, realistically you are not going to change your employer's practices. Rather than fight it, figure out who is in the know about jobs. Get to know these people. Let them know what you may be interested in for the future. Appeal to their desire to help someone else. They will be doing a service to you and performing "an act of goodness" to share this information with you.

Learn from how others did it. Ask around, look around, and read through your company literature, press releases, senior management speeches, and whatever you can glean information from. Try to determine who within your organization has had a career path similar to what you think you want. Contact these people. Again, ask to meet with them, conduct informational interviews with them, and ascertain if they would be willing to be an informal mentor to you.

Enlist a mentor. The norm is that a mentor is more powerful—someone more senior than you who has the ability in the organization to share wisdom with you, champion you in the organization, run interference, and so on. Often, there are only a handful of these executives and everyone is clamoring for their time.

I advise you to seek out the unconventional mentor. This could even be a peer—a star on the rise, someone who will tell it like it is and support you and vice versa. You can figure career paths out together and help each other as you both move sideways or up, as you aspire to.

Volunteer for a project or committee. Give your time and talents to a group you are interested in learning more about, such as a company-wide task force that involves a great group of people. Or volunteer for the team that's setting up the annual holiday or summer event. You'll meet new people, widening your circle of contacts, as well as gain recognition for a job well done.

Design Your Own Career Path

Study the organization chart. What are the jobs at the highest levels? What are the functional areas/departments/groups? What are the titles? Who are the people in these jobs? The good old organization chart is a font of information for key groups and departments and how they fit together, who the important players are, and the kinds of top jobs to which you can aspire.

Outline your path. Review the organization chart to understand the natural or typical progression of jobs and roles that could lead you to the top spot (the destination job) that you aspire to. Do your own sort of succession planning. Look at where you are now in the organization. Your name probably won't show up on the organization chart, but which group or box are you in? Where do you think you want to be in three years, five years, ten years at this company or one like it? What are the successive next steps, next career moves you can take to get where you wish to go? You are essentially designing some career paths for yourself and determining what steps you need to take on the journey and to reach the destination.

Let's say that you'd like to be the COO (chief operating officer) one day. You take a look at the organization chart and see that the groups and boxes reporting to that position are Finance, Human Resources, Accounting and Compliance, Operations, and so on. A good start for a career path would be that you try for a job in each one of these areas, so that you build a strong base of experience, knowledge, skills, and relationships.

Knit together the best roles for you. The best jobs or roles are those that:

- Don't get hung up on title or level
- Provide you challenging responsibilities that will expand your experience base and build new skills and strengths
- Come with a supportive manager who will help (or at least not hinder) your career development, even if it is you who is guiding it

- Enable you to learn from your manager and the people with whom you interact
- Give you visibility; go for the jobs and roles that offer you the chance to take some risks, make significant contributions to the organization
- Engage you to stay around a while; try for the jobs where you will stay motivated and stimulated in the role long enough to initiate and implement new ideas, positive changes, a process, project, and so on
- Allow time for on-the-side projects, committees, task forces, programs, and formal and informal learning opportunities that will supplement your job to further build your knowledge and competencies

Make your own plan and follow it. Contact a manager at the highest level possible in each of the groups you are interested in. Tell the person that you would appreciate the chance to learn more about what he does. Ask to meet with the manager. Treat this as an informational interview. Find out about his background, key challenges and content of the work, how he got to that place, what typical jobs are along the career path, and how you can improve your potential of moving over to that area. (Refer to Chapter 4 for questions in an informational interview.) If you have hit it off, at the end of your meeting, ask if you could continue to seek his help or advice periodically. Voilà, you have an informal mentor in the organization!

Establish Career Tools for a Lifetime

Develop a career advisory board. Recruit three to five people you respect to serve on your own personal career advisory board. Choose those you can go to for career advice, support, referrals, and references, or to bounce ideas off. Select a different person for each of your needs so you can have the broadest insights. For example, you may want to enlist one person who is senior and an industry expert, someone who is an ace at job searches, another person who knows you well and can keep you honest with yourself, and a former manager who is wise about most anything.

Consult your career advisory board at strategic points in your career.

These are times when you are switching jobs or changing careers, when something is not working for you, when you are considering taking a big risk, when you are facing an ethical dilemma, or when you are dealing with any of the challenges presented in this book.

Recession-proof your career. There are always ways you can be developing yourself and your career. To recession-proof your career, you need to continually improve your skills and gain new skills and competencies so that you remain employable, marketable, and competitive. This is called "owning" your career and career development over your entire work lifetime. In my dealings with recruiters and senior executives who choose their successors, there seems to be a common set of skills and competencies that we need today to thrive in our careers. Take a look at the career toolkit in Figure 12-1.

● TOOLS AND RESOURCES

Career Toolkit

The nine knowledge areas, skills, and abilities in the career toolkit are essential competencies for you to develop over time. They provide a diverse and resilient toolkit of strengths that you can take with you whatever your job or career path.

A Roadmap: Actualization and Transcendence in Your Career

The ideal, the ultimate in developing your career over a lifetime—whether you choose to have many careers and jobs or to work in a few key positions—is actualization and transcendence. Maslow's Hierarchy of Needs is a popular view of this and is frequently cited as a theory of human motivation. Often represented by a pyramid, the Hierarchy of Needs has the basic premise that there are levels of human needs that must be met before an individual can reach the highest level of wisdom and consciousness—that of self-actualization. Self-actualized people are those who realize self-fulfillment and their potential.

The career metaphor for each of Maslow's eight levels (see Figure

Figure 12-1. Career Toolkit

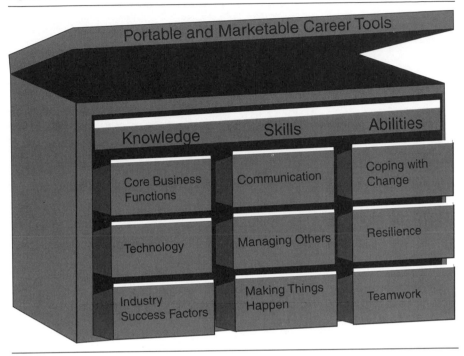

12-2) moves you from the basics of finding a job to the ultimate aspiration of managing your career strategically over your lifetime.

A person must attain each successive level of needs before being able to progress to the next level. Starting at the bottom of the pyramid with physiological needs, one can keep reaching the highest level needs. The pinnacle in the hierarchy of needs is for an individual to reach self-actualization, then transcendence, helping others realize their fulfillment and their potential.

Clarifying and following your purpose and path as you develop your career over your lifetime allows you the ultimate in your career: to realize your career actualization and transcendence. Most of us never make it quite to the top, but the journey is a stimulating and gratifying adventure.

For each of Maslow's level of needs, there is a career metaphor—what an actualized and transcended career would look like and achieve. We draw on an extended version of eight levels of needs, further delineated from the common five. At the bottom, the base, would be to have a job that pays.

Figure 12-2. Career-Related Metaphors for Maslow's Hierarchy

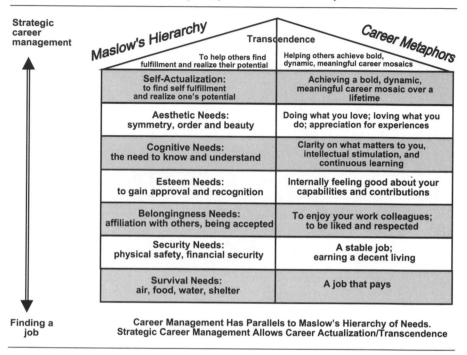

Career Management Has Parallels to Maslow's Hierarchy of Needs.
Strategic Career Management Allows Career Actualization/Transcendence

The highest level of wisdom and consciousness—of career actualization and then transcendence—would be to achieve a bold, meaningful, dynamic career over a lifetime and to help others along the way on their journeys. It would mean to do work that matters to you and that you enjoy, to continuously learn and develop yourself, and to send the elevator back down for others when you've reached your highest level.

Coping with Unethical Conduct

HAVE YOU EVER BEEN ASKED to "cook the books," misrepresent facts or figures to make the company look better, or tell a white lie to obtain more favorable terms in a negotiation? Have you been privy to colleagues or higher-ups' "borrowing" company property for their private use, padding their expense accounts, or operating in a gray area of company policy for their own advantage? Have you discovered that one of your staff took a few sick days off to interview for another job or go away for a long weekend? Have you heard about a senior manager who used the company jet to go far out of the way to get crab dinners for his family on the way home from the East Coast? Perhaps your CEO used a heavy hand, stepping outside of company guidelines to gain unfair concessions for using labor in a Third World country? Maybe you heard your boss ask his administrative assistant to lie to his wife to cover up an extramarital affair.

● DEFINING THE CHALLENGE

The above are all examples of ethical dilemmas. You found out about an action or a behavior that may be considered unethical. What do you do about it? There are numerous technical definitions of ethics. Put simply, in a business and workplace context, an action or behavior in violation of stated company policy, values, or code of conduct is unethical. Most of us would also agree, however, that there have been or will be times when we think an action is unethical even though it may be within the letter of the law or company policy.

This is because each of us possesses our own set of ethics—an internal compass that guides our actions and behaviors on a day-to-day basis. We each adhere to a unique combination of values, morals, and judgments about what we consider right or wrong. Our personal ethics may actually be stricter or looser than those considered sacrosanct by employers or the workplace culture.

Unethical behavior can come from anyone, anywhere, anytime. The CEO or an executive, your own manager, one of your staff, a coworker, a strategic partner, or a vendor may engage in unethical behavior. The act may be a one-time incident, occur as regular episodes, or be ongoing. It can range from "small stuff" to "off the charts" in seriousness to the organization.

● FACING THE CHALLENGE

With the media attention on the goings-on at companies like Enron, there's a deeper awareness and much discussion about what's ethical and what's not. Many of us have already faced or will face in our lifetime the challenge of dealing with an unethical higher-up, colleague, or subordinate. What we would do is not as cut-and-dried as one might think, especially when a job, a career, or a valued reputation is at stake. This chapter will discuss strategies, tips, and advice for how to approach the problem of people in your workplace who are clearly, or not so clearly, doing something unethical.

Decoding the Unethical Act

Get the facts. Make sure you observe or know firsthand what the person actually did that you think may be unethical. Review company policy. Assess whether the action or behavior is breaking company policy, violates its code of conduct, or is an act against its values. Note that especially if you are new to the industry, to the company, or to your particular work group, there may be practices that don't seem right but are accepted company or industry norms.

For example, you may work for one employer where it is considered a violation of policy to accept any gift from a vendor. This could be lunch, tickets to a sports event, or a box of candy. In another industry or company, this may be perfectly acceptable as long as you either share the gift with your colleagues or report it somehow. You may work in one group in which the manager allows her staff to take sick days when they aren't sick. Another manager may consider this practice unacceptable and as falsifying company records. Know the facts. Understand what you are dealing with.

Make sure the deed warrants action. Use your judgment and common sense about how to proceed. In an ideal world you would be able to talk with the person directly and persuade her to stop doing whatever it is. There will also be times when you may choose not to do anything to follow up.

For example, if the person is stealing paper clips, you will need to decide if it is worth the effort or potential rift in your relationship to talk with the person directly or to tell someone else, such as the manager or HR. A person stealing paper clips, padding an expense account, or using a cell phone for personal calls may be distasteful to your code of ethics and technically in violation of company policy, but you must decide if the deeds warrant your outing the person.

This is something only you can decide. In coaching clients, I usually suggest using the "bringing-down-the-company" test. Not to sound overly dramatic, but this means taking a close look at the ramifications of the situation. Is what the person doing something materially detrimental to the company? Will it negatively impact the company's bottom line? Will it harm the company's reputation in the market, make it go out of business, lose millions of dollars, or harm its customers? Sometimes it's difficult to assess this yourself and you will need to seek the advice and counsel of a mentor or someone who can help, either inside or outside the organization.

Risky Business

Assess the risk. Coming forward with information on unethical conduct will always present some risk. Not telling also involves risk. Assess how much risk there is and if it is something you are willing to take on. Here are some questions to guide your thinking:

- What are the likely scenarios if you come forward with the information? For example, one scenario is that HR could start an investigation, you and others will be called upon as witnesses, and the person ultimately gets put on probation or fired.

- What could happen to you and your job, your reputation, your career? For example, the person you expose could try and place the blame on you or make you the scapegoat.

List the possible outcomes and estimate the probability of each occurring. Also, consider what could happen if you don't tell what you know. List the possible outcomes if you keep quiet. What is the probability of each of those outcomes? Could you live with yourself if the worst possible outcome happened?

Now you have a pretty clear picture of what you are dealing with and how high or low the risk is of something potentially bad or good happening because of your coming forward. Factor this into your assessment of how strongly you believe that something must be done about the unethical behavior and how potentially harmful the effect could be if nothing is done. (The last section of this chapter will help you take yourself through a more in-depth risk assessment.)

Evaluate if coming forward with the information is worth the risk. In cases where there are serious unethical and even illegal activities going on, you may also have to consider the possibility of legal action against you for withholding what you knew if you don't come forward and/or the threat to your personal safety, or potential harm to you or your family, if you do come forward. You may need to consult an attorney or get expert advice on how to proceed.

Determine if it's a career-limiting move. For most people, the worst thing that can happen if they come forward and tell on the person would be to lose their jobs. Another possibility is being made the scapegoat—somehow getting blamed for all or part of the unethical action or behavior. Perhaps you'll be ostracized by the person you outed. Being retaliated against, or persecuted in some way, is another real possibility. Character assassination—having your character attacked or made questionable—is an example of this. Think long and hard about the consequences of coming forward with the information you know. In the end, you are your own judge of what the right thing is to do.

Coming Forward

Decide whom to tell. If your facts, risk assessment, and thoughtful evaluation lead you to decide to come forward with the information, you will need to determine whom to tell. Ideally, go to a powerful mentor or a well-respected senior manager with whom you have a close, trusting relationship. Ask for the person's advice on what to do and how to proceed.

The head of HR is another viable person to talk with about what you know and how to proceed. It should be a given, but to make yourself feel better, make sure you have his complete confidentiality. Before you go into the details, let the HR person know that what you want to discuss is sensitive and difficult. Usually HR has people with experience and valuable expertise to listen to what you have to say, investigate it without accusing the other person, and determine what should be done. You need to remember as well that, out of respect to that person, HR or whoever is looking into the situation will not keep you posted on everything being done or what is going on. Investigations take time; keep in mind that the person you are outing is considered innocent until proven guilty.

Exit Strategies

Go outside if you need to. If no one you tell in the company will do anything and you believe what is going on is serious, unethical, and illegal, then seek advice from an attorney or someone who knows the laws for your industry or situation. The EEOC (Equal Employment Opportunity Commission), the SEC (Securities and Exchange Commission), the FDA (Food and Drug Administration), the SAG (Screen Actors Guild), and the FASB (Financial Accounting Standards Board) are examples of agencies, commissions, and groups that are expert for specific areas of practices and laws. Many industries and professions also have ethics or standards boards.

Transfer within the company. The best-case scenario is that you have talked with the appropriate people in the company and they are handling it from there (investigating and following up as appropriate with the person involved). If you feel that you can't be around or work with the person you reported, try to make a move within the company as soon as possible. Ask for support and help from either HR or your manager. This approach has worked out for many people, especially if they enjoy most other aspects of the organization and are highly invested in their careers and thus would prefer not to have to leave. Sometimes extricating yourself from the person you reported is enough to allow you to move on. Sometimes it's not.

Leave the company. If ultimately nothing is done to the person or there only is a "slap on the wrist," decide whether what has happened is in such conflict with your own value system and beliefs that you have to leave the company. If you decide to leave, first make sure you have a cash reserve—a safety net while you look for another job. Another option is to stay in your job and hang in there while discreetly beginning a job search. You can resign and give notice when you land another job.

A third option is to speak with HR and let that department know that you are uncomfortable staying in the organization given what has transpired. Ask if you can be moved to another part of the company (perhaps a sister operating company or a division in a new location) or be given some kind of career transition help (severance of sorts, outplacement services, an agreement that you will receive fair and favorable references, etc.). Handle the request firmly and amicably, not with threats of exposing the company or the person.

Take the high road. When you are interviewing and people ask you why you are considering a move, determine what you will say. Taking the high road and remaining classy is usually the best. You could say "I'm ready for a new challenge" or something like "There are some philosophical or ethical differences with someone in my former company. My own values and belief system made it uncomfortable for me to stay there." You don't want to sound preachy, but you do want to communicate why you needed to leave and also why the references coming from your former employer may not be the most glowing.

● TOOLS AND RESOURCES

A Risk Assessment Exercise

Take yourself through the following questions to get a sense of how risky it is to come forward with your information. This exercise probably will not change your mind about what you do, but it could engender more savvy thinking about how you do it.

- Is yours an open organizational culture, meaning that there's little hierarchy and a level playing field for all employees to say what's on their minds?
- Does management accept honest, direct feedback or criticism from employees?
- Is HR fair and equitable in dealing with all levels of employees, not just acting as management advocates?
- What have you seen happen to others who have come forward with information about unethical behavior?
- Are there urban legends or stories about the messenger getting shot or nothing ever being done?
- How powerful or entrenched is the person you will be outing?
- What is her likely reaction to your exposure?
- What backups, reinforcements, or help can you rely on if you need to? These may be inside or outside the organization.

Being Fired or Pushed Out

HAVE YOU BEEN FIRED seemingly for no reason? Was it out of the blue and not part of a larger layoff or reorganization? Do you have a suspicion that your boss or a higher-up doesn't like you or is looking for a way to get rid of you? Has your manager been hypercritical lately, finding fault with most everything you do and giving you a poor performance review that you felt was unfair? For example, did your manager fixate on one or two things you did wrong and generalize it to the rest of your review? Have you had good performance reviews until now and this one seems to come out of left field? Does your manager appear to be insecure about his own job or seem threatened by your successes or just doesn't like you? Do you have a new CEO or senior manager who has been bringing her own team into the organization, and there's writing on the wall that the old guard will be pushed out?

● DEFINING THE CHALLENGE

There are many reasons you could be fired or pushed out of your job. This chapter does not address the times and situations when your employer's business needs or your job performance truly warrant it. For example, being fired or being pushed out may be appropriate when the business is doing poorly and difficult cutbacks must be made; when a whole group or function must be outsourced (done by a more cost-effective set of employees) to keep the organization competitive; when an employee's skills have become obsolete or his or her performance is consistently subpar; or when someone is widely viewed as impossible to work with, has made some disastrous missteps, caused major damage to the employer's business or reputation, violated a company policy or ethics code, or is not on board with the vision and direction of the company and is a constant roadblock to change. The list goes on and on.

There are times, however, when a manager may want to get rid of an employee, either through an outright firing or with the semblance of a fairer process such as giving poor performance reviews or placing the employee on a corrective action of some sort. Corrective actions may have other company-specific names, but essentially they are a process by which you get placed on notice for something you may have done wrong, have underperformed, or are deficient in some way.

Your manager must outline clear steps that you must take to correct what is wrong. The manager is also supposed to give you adequate time for making the improvements. Many companies have three steps to corrective actions. For example, the first stage of being placed on corrective action is notification. Being moved to the next step for not successfully making the changes puts you on probation. If after the allotted time you still have not succeeded in the corrective actions, the final step is termination.

● FACING THE CHALLENGE

From having the unpleasant task of firing people over the years, coaching managers on how to do it, and helping employees rebound from being fired, I must note that employers are usually aboveboard and thoughtful about whom they have to fire and why. First, companies—especially those with deep pockets—are risk-averse when it comes to firing employees. They can be sued if there's a hint of discrimination, constructive discharge, or not acting in "good faith." Second, their reputations are at stake. An egregious firing, even at a low (not senior) level, can make the news, bring unwanted attention to the organization, and cause public distrust. Third, employers usually fire for good reason because of the potential negative implications on employee morale. If their employees see another employee mistreated—even if he or she is not liked—the employees will lose respect for their employer and begin to think that they could be next.

This chapter discusses the times when your being fired or pushed out is not really fair or warranted and when there is something you may be able to do to keep your job or at least to improve your situation. We focus on the times when there is a chance to reverse the direction things are moving in or, at minimum, to create some positive outcome for yourself.

Some Basic Facts on Firings

Most companies are "at will" employers, meaning that they can hire or fire you at will, with or without cause. Even so, technically, they cannot fire you if, in doing so, they violate basic tenets, such as discrimination on the basis of race, gender, age, ethnicity, religious beliefs, or sexual orientation. When companies fire someone and it's not really warranted, they typically operate in the gray areas—situations that are often open to subjective interpretation and therefore some manipulation or spin. These can be divided into the whys and the hows.

Common reasons *why* someone gets fired when it may not be warranted are:

- You've been outspoken about management or the company and are seen as a troublemaker.
- You make too much money and it would be cheaper to bring in less experienced, younger, hungrier talent.
- You have lost a powerful mentor and are now on the "outs" or you have been on the losing side of a political battle.
- Your manager is jealous of you personally or professionally or in some way views you as a threat.
- A new manager comes in and sees you as the old guard and possibly part of the problems of the old regime.
- You have had personal problems and are dragging your team and/ or manager down because of excessive absenteeism, unpredictable emotional outbursts, or not being completely focused on your job.
- You are a roadblock to change and seem critical about any new ideas that management institutes.
- You are not respected for whatever reason.
- You are not liked for whatever reason.

The *hows* of what the company will say in order to fire you will be under the guise of "business need." They include:

- Your job is eliminated. It either will go completely unfilled, say for at least a year, or it will be redesigned and the qualifications needed for the new position will not be the same as yours.
- You are underperforming. You did not reach your goals and objectives or have had declining performance.
- Because you did X, Y, and Z, you are placed you on corrective action, with steps and a timeline to fix the problems. When you do not make the improvements in your manager's viewpoint, you will be terminated.
- Your customers, peers, or staff have complained about you.
- You make too much and your manager will say the company cannot afford to keep you on.

The means by which your employer would fire you or push you out are typically: two weeks' pay in lieu of notice, a corrective action, one very bad performance review, declining performance reviews, or confidential talks that make it clear the employer wants you to leave.

You're Fired! (or About to Be)

See being fired and doing something about it as a chess match or as a challenge to be tackled. Being fired or pushed out can deal you a devastating personal blow, but you need to detach your emotions as much as possible and keep your wits about you. You need to remain clearheaded about what you need to do and thoughtful in your implementation.

Decide if it's worth the fight. Ask yourself if you really want to stay with this manager or in this company or if you have wanted to leave for a while anyway. If you've needed a nudge to walk out the door, accept the firing or being pushed out and move on.

Maximize your severance and career transition assistance. If you have been fired or are on your way to it, think of negotiation points for as generous as possible a severance package and career transition help. Severance pay is usually offered by medium to large companies based on years of service. One or two weeks of your normal salary or pay per year of service is the norm, with some sort of maximum amount. If you have been offered severance, see what you can do to get more. If you work for a small employer that does not offer severance, ask for it. Provide the reasons you deserve it and offer some creative ways your employer can help you. Some examples for how to build a persuasive case are at the end of the chapter.

Keep your approach and tactics professional, never threatening, but don't be afraid to push the envelope. The old adage "Ask and you shall receive" is often the case. Most employers that fire someone, even if it was for dubious reasons, will want to try to do something to help the employee. Sometimes they even will feel some guilt, so you should not be shy about asking for assistance. The tipping points for employers are if what you're asking for (1) is reasonable, (2) is within their resources, (3) would not be seen as ludicrous or unfair if other employees got wind of the deal, and (4) won't be used against them if they vary from what they've done in the past—that is, that you won't come back and sue them anyway.

Seek legal counsel, if warranted. Consider, not lightly, an attorney well versed in employment law. If you truly think you have been wrongly fired or are being pushed out unfairly, you could talk with an attorney to see what, if any, case you have, the likelihood of success (settlement, reinstatement of your job, or a move to another job within the company), and estimated legal fees. Often attorneys will work on a contingency basis and not take your case unless they believe it is a strong one. The reason I advise not to take this option lightly is that in lawsuits there is really never a winner. Both sides are dragged down into negativity, reputations are hurt, and you may not be able to move on with your career or life with this looming over you. There are times, however, when a lawsuit may be appropriate, especially if it will help others not suffer the same fate or if you have really been mistreated.

Determine what you want. Figure out what you can do and what a successful outcome would be for you. Try to ascertain what you can do, how much effort it will take, how you will define a good outcome, the likelihood of success, and whether it's easier to just walk away—try another manager, group, or even employer. If you were fired, at best you could maximize your severance pay or career transition assistance or your job could be reinstated. If you are being pushed out and your efforts succeed, you might be able to keep your job, work elsewhere in the company for a manager who appreciates you, or expose your manager as the problem.

Fess up to what you've done wrong and offer to fix it. If there is something you've done wrong or could have done better on, then admit it. Say how you plan to fix it, offer a plan with realistic steps and timing, and ask for another chance to prove yourself. Then work so hard that you exceed your promise. You might need to take a course on your own time; work overtime; get some help from a coach, Human Resources, a mentor, or a friend who has the expertise you need; read every book you can get your hands on, and so on.

Evaluate the "threats." Who and what can undermine or render ineffective what you will try to do? Where are the vulnerable spots in which someone or something could hurt your efforts? Identify ways to offset those. For example:

- If your boss truly has an agenda and nothing you could do would really change that, then think about those people who are not enamored with your boss. Usually bosses like this have created their own enemies. Their own bosses could often have some suspicions about them. Enlist the assistance of his or her boss if you feel you would be believed or helped. Go to Human Resources in confidence. Tell HR why you believe you are being treated unfairly and ask for advice or intervention.
- Call on someone who knows you well and knows your work. This could be a well-respected manager in a different group from yours who would be willing to make a position for you on his team or talk with your manager about giving you a chance to improve. This would at least buy you some time to look for another job within the company or elsewhere and still be employed, bringing in an income.
- Try to counter every negative with a positive. Methodically take each bad thing being said about you and find people (champions or those willing

to stand up with the truth), facts, figures, reports, anecdotal evidence, or tangible items that challenge it, disprove it, or dispel the negative. For example, if it's being said that you were the lowest performer in sales revenues over the last quarter, but usually sales performance is viewed over a year and you still have time to go, make a case for how the company has typically evaluated the whole year and not just one quarter. If it's being said that you are difficult to work with, try to find the people who think otherwise. If one or two people did say this but *they* are difficult to work with and your boss is just using it against you, go to those people and appeal to their sense of goodness. Tell them you understand there have been some difficulties in working together and figure out together how you can make it better. If you can go back to your boss and tell her that you have taken active steps to fix the problem, that makes it more difficult to use as a basis for firing or in a performance review against you.

Seek out others' help and support. Enlist advice or help from friends, coworkers, and others in the organization who are supportive. Ask for what you need—an empathetic sounding board, a head-clearing or uplifting diversion, some problem solving on what steps to take, and so on.

Disagreeing with Your Performance Review

Keep in mind that your review stays with you as long as you are in the company. If someone gives you a performance review that is unfair or misrepresentative, it will be in your file until the day you leave. Your future managers will see the review. It will come into play when you are being considered for other opportunities, promotions, raises, even succession or developmental planning.

Make time for your part of the review. Always take considerable time and thought to fill out the "employee comments" section of your review. This is not a throwaway section, and you should never be too busy to do it. Mitigate potential comments you may disagree with by giving thorough consideration to what you say in your employee comments. You don't have to write a book, but be clear and compelling about what you have accomplished during the review period. (A simple outline or worksheet for developing your comments is provided at the end of this chapter.) If the performance appraisal form or process does not allow you to provide your self-assessment comments, you can take the initiative to write something up as an attachment and discuss the comments with your manager during the review.

Too often, I hear clients who have had bad or shocking reviews say they were too busy to write something, or that they don't like to "toot their own horns," or that they assumed their managers would be fair and knowledgeable about what they did. To these excuses I would say:

- Evaluating and communicating what you have achieved is just as important as any other project or work activity and certainly has direct, important implications for you.
- There is a difference between tooting your horn and being objective and truthful about your performance.
- Many managers consider performance evaluations a nuisance, waste of time, or something they are not good at. They may not be interested or incented to do a thorough job on them.
- You know best what you actually accomplished and have the biggest stake in making sure the review reflects both positives as well as where you need to develop or improve.

Refer to your agreed-upon goals, objectives, and priorities. Offer specific facts, figures when possible, and anecdotal examples on how you performed on each. At the beginning of a new year or new job or change in responsibilities, you and your manager should have discussed what's expected of you and how you will measure it. If you can't get your manager to discuss goals, objectives, and priorities, then at least write up what you think they should be. Give your manager a copy and keep a copy for yourself. Use these as a basis for your self-review.

Pay close attention. In the review, listen carefully and jot notes when you do not agree with what your manager is saying. Rather than interrupt, let him go through the whole review so you get a sense for the review in total.

Just say no. If there are serious disagreements about your performance, tell your manager you do not agree with his assessment. Indicate in general where. Say that you need time to process the information. Ask that you meet again in a few days.

Make your case. In your next meeting, focus calmly but firmly on the areas of disagreement. Give counterpoints to what your manager says. Use objective data—facts, figures, examples, and specifics—making your case on your view of your performance in the areas in question.

Ask that your manager change his assessment on the areas you disagree with or ask that you be able to include an addendum noting why you do not agree with certain portions of the review.

Seek other opinions. Be ready to call on people who will vouch for your performance. Get influential people or those who know your work to come to your defense. Ask them to write a brief paragraph or bullet points to outline their experience in working with you and how they viewed your performance. They can send it as an e-mail or letter for you to use as evidence for your defense.

Get help from Human Resources if you need it. Human Resources is supposed to be the best arbiter for disagreements regarding performance appraisals. Talk with someone there; explain rationally and calmly why you disagree; ask for the person's advice on how best to handle the situation. Sometimes you'll want to connect with the person before you do anything further with your manager. Use your judgment on whether it is best to bring the HR person in only after you have tried discussing the situation with your manager.

Contesting a Corrective Action

Nip it in the bud! This is a very tricky topic because your actions would be very different if you believe you were going to be given a fair chance to correct your mistakes versus if you believe that your manager is using this tool as a way to get rid of you. If the corrective action were really being used for its true purpose, you would correct what needs to be fixed, get off of corrective action, and continue in your job. We are going to assume for our purposes that you are being placed on corrective action unfairly. The first order of advice, then, is to disagree with the action. Make a note of it for your file. Find evidence—facts, figures, examples, and people who will vouch for you.

Ask for intervention. Go to your manager's manager or HR (Employee Relations or the head of HR) and ask for the person to step in. Tell the individual that you do not agree with your being placed on corrective action. Remember that HR and your manager's manager may well be aware of what is going on and may fully support it, so be prepared not to get this person's help or to be told that she upholds your manager's view.

Take corrective action and document it. If you are unable to get yourself removed from corrective action, then try to make sure that you can do the steps being outlined as the ones you need to take to correct your performance issue or mistake. Usually in a corrective action, you will need to take certain steps within a specified amount of time. For example, you may have three steps to a corrective action: (1) notification and 30 days to fix what's wrong; (2) another 30 days to take the corrective action if you have not already done it, or move to a probationary period; and (3) if you have not corrected things by those next 30 days, you move to termination. You want to succeed in the outlined steps as early in the process as possible so you won't be moved to the next stage. If you are performing what is outlined in the corrective action, then technically you cannot be moved to the next stage and should be removed from corrective action.

Realize it's not over. If you are effective in getting off your corrective action, it's not the end of your challenge. A manager who wants to get rid of you will try other ways. Be thankful that your efforts saved you this time, but begin planning your strategy. You'll need to think about how you will defend yourself from your manager's attempts (a defensive strategy) or plan something more proactive (an offensive strategy) to keep this from happening again.

　　Defensive tactics include keeping your performance high; developing important 360-degree relationships with people (your higher-ups, peers, staff/customers) who like and respect you and know the quality of your work; and taking HR as a partner and keeping that department in the loop confidentially on how you are trying to take the high road to work with your manager, but still informing HR periodically of what your manager is doing.

Offensive tactics include moving to another group with a manager who will appreciate and develop you; having a heart-to-heart with your manager and letting her know that however you got off on the wrong foot, you really want to be a great team and get along or work to achieve the group's success; and lobbying to get rid of your manager if she is the real problem.

Expose your manager as the real problem. This would be the most difficult to do, but consider it as ridding your organization of the actual problem, if this is the case. While this is highly unusual, it has been done, especially if the manager has made enemies, is disrespected, or has taken missteps. If the manager is not performing well, is not respected or liked, and/or has a reputation for not treating other colleagues or his own staff fairly, chances are you may be able to influence the manager's being moved elsewhere or out of the company. You'll need to seek out others who have issues with the manager and discreetly determine if they are willing to join you in bringing the manager's shortcomings to light. Ascertain the level of support your manager has with his own manager and HR, as well as with senior management. If the support is shaky, your and others' complaints about the manager may be what HR or your manager's manager needs to get him to leave.

Don't attack your manager or go on a campaign against him. And never say anything dishonest. People will think less of you. Even if you succeed in getting your boss moved to another job or out of the company, you will be distrusted and scrutinized as to how you deal with your next boss. Use facts, figures, and other people's experiences as well as your own to build your case of why your manager is the problem. Ask that something be done. You are not on a mission to harm your manager's reputation or inflict personal hurt. Remember that this is a last-resort effort; you should undertake it only if your manager really is a problem and something should be done about it for the good of others and your organization.

Be prepared to leave if your strategy doesn't work. If your manager is talked to and put on notice but remains in his position, you've pretty much exhausted your resources. You'll need to go to Plan B—move either to another group or out of the company.

Keeping from Being Pushed Out by a New Manager

Don't demonize the new manager. When a new senior manager or CEO wants to bring in her own team, this is not an unreasonable effort. Often, the manager may believe that doing this in key positions or doing it more widely will help turn around the company or grow the business the fastest. The manager has a trusted and established relationship with the people she wants to bring in or perhaps simply believes these other people outside the organization are the best at what they do and represent what the organization needs now.

Sometimes, however, a new senior manager may arrive and without careful consideration or due diligence will want to get rid of what she considers the old guard—the employees considered part of the problem or of the old regime that caused the company to do poorly. Here are some suggestions for this situation.

Meet with the new manager. Schedule a meeting with the new senior manager. Introduce yourself, welcome the person, and let her know that you are willing to be a resource. If you have already met the individual and have been given the cold shoulder, schedule a meeting on the pretext of talking about a particular challenge or issue to resolve.

Remember that you are being evaluated. Your meeting with this new manager will be an evaluation, so go in 100 percent prepared. This is a time when you want to put your best foot forward or correct any misconceptions about yourself.

Think about the impression you want to make. Decide on the two or three compelling points you want to make about what you are doing in the company and why your contribution is important. Be ready to cover high-level or detailed questions or issues about your responsibilities or your group. Bring some selective examples of your work to the meeting just in case it is appropriate to show them.

Prepare for your being asked to leave. The senior manager may make clear to you that he would like you to consider leaving the organization whether or not you have initiated the meeting. Know in advance what you will say by creating some talking points beforehand. Some ideas are in the last section of this chapter.

Demonstrate your value. Prove your value to the new senior manager with your actions. Let your performance speak loud and clear about why you are a keeper and valuable to the organization and to the manager. Keep doing a great job.

Create regular opportunities to show your stuff to the manager. Invite her to your staff meeting, the launch of a new project, or a celebration for your team for something you all have done well. Send periodic brief e-mails as you get positive feedback or results you can share.

Don't keep your head down. Make sure you are visible, your results and achievements are visible, and that, more than ever, your champions are vocal about you as an important player in the organization.

Assess your detractors and your supporters. Determine if a move to a different group, where the senior manager knows and supports you, is viable. A viable strategy is to make a move, then continue to perform well and thrive. You can eventually make a supporter out of the senior manager who has the time to see you in action, even from afar. Also, if you wait out the intense period when the new senior manager may be "cleaning house" and replacing people, you'll be in a better position.

● TOOLS AND RESOURCES

Outline for the Employee Comments Section of the Performance Review

Follow these five steps in completing the Performance Appraisal Worksheet (Figure 14-1):

1. Begin with a summary two to five sentences about what you accomplished and how it contributed to the overall success or achievements of your group or the company.

Figure 14-1. Performance Appraisal: Employee Comments Worksheet

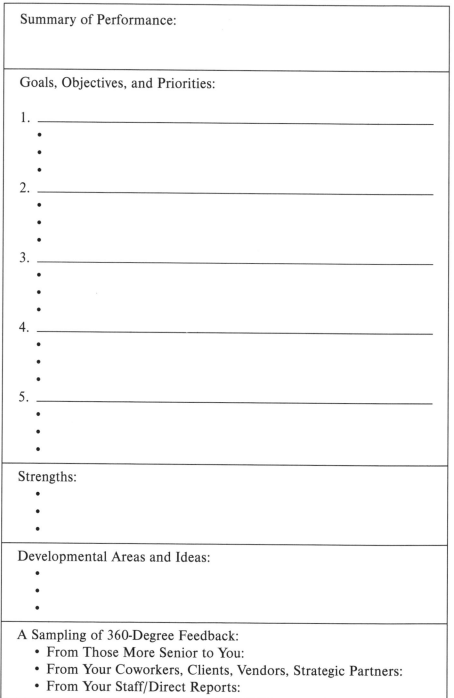

Summary of Performance:

Goals, Objectives, and Priorities:

1. _____
   •
   •
   •
2. _____
   •
   •
   •
3. _____
   •
   •
   •
4. _____
   •
   •
   •
5. _____
   •
   •
   •

Strengths:
   •
   •
   •

Developmental Areas and Ideas:
   •
   •
   •

A Sampling of 360-Degree Feedback:
   • From Those More Senior to You:
   • From Your Coworkers, Clients, Vendors, Strategic Partners:
   • From Your Staff/Direct Reports:

2. Use your goals, objectives, and priorities that were set and agreed upon with your manager as headings. Under each, develop two or three bullet points with facts, figures, or anecdotal examples of how you performed and what you accomplished.

3. Include a section calling out your strengths.

4. List some areas you would like to develop ("developmental areas") with a few ideas on how you can do that.

5. Provide samples of 360-degree feedback you've received. Include your own sampling of positive notes, e-mails, comments, feedback, survey ratings—whatever feedback you have heard from those you have worked with over the period being reviewed. These should represent those who are in roles more senior to you, your coworkers, clients, vendors, strategic partners, your staff or direct reports, and others with whom you work.

Negotiating More Severance Pay and/or Career Transition Help

Use the following suggestions to make a strong case:

- Make a case for why you deserve or need more than what they are offering. If it's a "one-off" firing (not being done to a group of people or a department), you could try to make a case for why you deserve or need more severance than usual: the job market is tight, you are older and there is a lot of competition for jobs, you will need to learn new skills, and so on.

- Make it personal if you think it will help your cause. Try to keep it based on business reasons but sometimes appealing to your manager, his or her manager, or Human Resources about your personal situation will be effective as well. If you've recently had a baby, are caring for a sick parent, just bought a house, or are supporting your son or daughter through a difficult time, share this information with them and see what they can do to offer the maximum assistance.

- Even if the company does not offer severance, be bold and ask for it. The company will be reluctant because it will set precedence for how it treats others after you. Try not calling it "severance." Instead, appeal to the powers that be (the CEO, your manager, someone in HR) that you need some sort of financial and career "assistance" to get on your feet. Tell them that this firing has been a surprise, a big blow to you, and that you will need time to get through this and need their help. Ask for creative options such as allowing you to stay on the payroll for a few weeks to a few months while you look for another job. Ask if they will pay for a course or career coach for you. Find out what they can do.

Preparation for Being Asked to Leave

Eliminate the surprise. Consider the following if you suspect you will be let go:

- Think about why you would be asked to leave.
- Consider what will be the stated reason and what may be the real, underlying ones.
- Reflect on the style of the manager. What might be persuasive to him; what are the hot buttons that could anger him; what have you seen work for others in interacting with this manager that you could adopt—for example, logic, emotion, humor, forcefulness, talking in metaphors or analogies, name dropping.
- Prepare how you will react to specific comments, what you could say, how you will handle the interaction in the worst-case scenario.

Surviving the Aftermath of a Merger or Acquisition

HAS YOUR COMPANY recently been acquired or merged with another company? If so, are most people you know, including yourself, feeling uncertain, anxious, or not sure about what to expect? Do you have a lot of questions on your mind? For example, will your job be eliminated or impacted in some way? What will happen next? What will it be like to work with the new management and the other employees of the other company? Who among your executive team will stay and who will go? What will happen to your boss, your colleagues, and the people you particularly enjoy working with? How will the culture, the values, and the way you all work together be impacted? Are there significant changes in store such as a turnabout in company strategy, direction, or priorities? Will there be layoffs and if so, massive or just cleaning house of "redundancies"? Will there be changes to your pay, health and other company benefits, or perks? Will the level of professional or career development you have be affected? How about the potential for career advancement opportunities—will these change, too?

● DEFINING THE CHALLENGE

There's no question that it can be unsettling to have your company taken over by or merged with another company. Rumors start flying, people start to speculate on what's coming, and often employees are given only tiny tidbits of information as overall plans are formulated. It's natural to feel confused, uncertain of the future, fearful of losing your job, and a number of other unpleasant emotions. Some people are crippled by these feelings, unable to carry on normally with their job. Others immediately start looking for another job without even waiting to hear what's going to happen. The resilient ones keep going to work, doing the best they can even as the changes begin to happen.

● FACING THE CHALLENGE

Most of what happens in the aftermath of a merger or acquisition is probably out of your control, so giving in to excessive worry and negative speculation is counterproductive. Yes, there will no doubt be changes, but you'll find it best to stay focused and involved in your work, keep abreast of the actual changes, not rumors, and deal with the changes that directly affect you and your job as they arise.

This chapter discusses dealing with the aftermath of a merger or acquisition from two perspectives:

1. If you are an individual contributor to mid-level manager
2. If you are a senior manager or playing a decision-making role in the merger or acquisition

Weathering the Storm

Wait and see. With most mergers or acquisitions, the reality is that it will take time for the organizations to integrate. It will take a while for the CEO and senior management to communicate major shifts in the merged company's strategy, direction, or priorities. Even if they are quick to lay this out, it will take time and effort for everyone to get on board and start moving in unison. So don't make any rash conclusions or decisions. Hang in there. Go with the flow. Wait and see what happens. With more information and more experience with the integrated organizations, you will be in a better position to decide what you want to do, particularly if you want to make a change in your job or leave the organization.

Develop a backup plan. Don't actively begin pursuing other job opportunities. However, now is as good a time as ever to start doing a few things that would help you make a move if you have to (if you're laid off) or want to (if you don't like the new direction or management). Give your résumé a complete, up-to-date makeover. Talk with some executive recruiter friends or other colleagues who may be hiring and discreetly ask them how the market looks for someone with your experience and background. In other words, quietly assess your employability.

Upgrade your skills. If there are skills or experience you are lacking or that you have let become rusty, take some focused time each week to work on bringing those up to par. In this way you will be more competitive if you do have to engage in a job search or career transition. Bringing your skills up to par may mean taking an evening course at your local community college, asking Human Resources to let you go to an in-house or outside program, or identifying someone inside or outside the organization whom you can apprentice with informally.

Stay alert. Don't be an ostrich. This is not the time to keep your head in the sand and be oblivious to what is going on around you. Pay attention to the communications issued "to the troops." What is being said? What's not being said? Take a critical look at the actions of the CEO, the executives, and Human Resources. What are they saying and, more important, what are they doing?

Proactive Strategies

Keep performing and producing. Now is not the time to slack off on your work or what you contribute. It is also not a good time to decrease your visibility. Anything you have been doing to perform well you need to keep on doing. If you can, rev it up a gear as well. You want to keep your good reputation as a talented, committed employee or manager. Stay focused and move forward full throttle.

Board the bus. You may have heard the phrase, "either get on the bus or get off of it." Make a conscious decision to support any new management and the changes they will make. If you can impact certain changes, then do that. Provide the reports or information that the new CEO or senior team needs. Initiate meetings with the new CEO or executive team members who will have direct or even indirect impact on you and your ability to perform your responsibilities. This may be a new head of a division or operating company or the CEO.

Insert yourself; include yourself; immerse yourself. Figure out what you can add to what's being done and how you can become invaluable to the new team. Ask what important meetings are coming up that you should be included in, lest you be left out. Not being included could have been an oversight, not a deliberate attempt to keep you out of the loop. In any event, invite yourself into the discussion and participate in the decisions being made.

You will need to use all of your powers of persuasion and outright charm, and then truly deliver what you promise. If you are not someone who will add value to the processes and discussions, then it will be evident pretty quickly to the new managers.

Know your value. What value—positive contribution—can you bring to the new or changed management team? For example, bring to the table your deep knowledge and experience, as well as your repertoire of positive working relationships. Could you offer one or more of the following if you found yourself in the aftermath of a merger or acquisition?

- Historical perspective/background—your intimate working knowledge of the company's operations, successes, failures, industry, and competitors; background for why you have made the decisions you have in the past and what has worked, what has not; key challenges, obstacles, what you need to be successful in your market space.
- Credibility and respect from the troops—are you respected and trusted by others in the organization—employees, peers, customers, vendors? Most savvy new management teams know that there are always opinion leaders, gatekeepers, bearers of the culture and the essence of the organization who are the key to getting everyone on board and moving in the right direction. Are you one of the pillars of the organization whom people will be watching to see how you react, what happens to or with you, and what you decide to do—whether to opt in or get out?

- Critical expertise—you may be the best at what you do or simply have so much experience doing what you have been doing with the organization that it would be a huge loss for you to leave. Are you indispensable?

Opt out. After letting the dust settle and assessing where the newly formed organization is going, decide if you want to opt in or out. Some of the main reasons I've seen people opt out are:

- The company is no longer a fit with their values—their belief system.
- They do not agree with the new company direction or strategy.
- Their jobs have changed so much and they don't like them any more—for example, new responsibilities or some taken away; new boss, different metrics, goals, or objectives that they don't agree with.
- They experience style or personality differences or clashes with the new CEO or executive team.
- They feel like an outsider or no matter what they do they are considered part of the old guard or are not included in the inner circle.
- They feel such deep allegiance and loyalty to the outgoing CEO or other executives who have left the company that it is difficult to get excited about performing in the new organization.
- It's a good time to stop, take some time off, and think about the next chapter in their careers—a good time for a change.

Playing a Role in the Transition

If you are a senior executive at a company that is undergoing a merger or acquisition, you can anticipate playing a role in the transition at some point. I have asked industry expert Andrew Miller, vice president of Finance and chief accounting officer for Autodesk, to offer insights and advice on dealing with this problem. Andrew has served on the senior management teams of companies such as Silicon Graphics, Cadence, and MarketFirst when they were merged or acquired.

A synopsis of what Andrew told me follows.

Know your priorities. It is a well-known fact that 70 to 80 percent of M&As fail to deliver the desired results (return on investment). My experience, based on 15 to 20 transactions across a few companies, supports this statistic. What separates the successes from the failures? A clear, explicit, and common understanding of what is expected from the transaction. First off, you must understand what is happening and why. Don't be afraid to ask questions of the new executive team right from the start. Why are you doing this? What are the value drivers? What are your expectations for the immediate future and for the longer term? What will be the impact on personnel?

The answers to questions like these will form the basis for how you should proceed. You'll know what you should attempt to preserve at all costs versus what you really don't have to care about. In my experience, this ruthless prioritization is often lost at many stages of the transaction and subsequent integration project, which dooms the project to failure. This is true not only for the overall company but also for you as an individual manager. If the project fails, you'll fail along with it.

The most common problem is losing sight of the value drivers and the return on investment anticipated by the acquiring company or by the senior managers of the merged organization. The aftermath of a merger or acquisition is a time to pay more attention than ever before to the bottom line, questioning everything as if you were seeing it for the first time.

A second problem occurs when, during the integration, you focus equally on all problems, as opposed to the critical few that you have to get right. I recall a particular transaction in one company in my past. We acquired another company for its semiconductor development team—this was the only reason to acquire the company. After the acquisition, a leader from elsewhere in our company was given responsibility for the development team. He moved his own people onto the team, displacing key incumbents. He didn't focus on retaining the key talent that he had just acquired and much of the new development team ended up leaving within one year. The result was that the chip was released to market more than one year late, negatively impacting the performance of the entire company.

Get aligned. Seek alignment across the senior team, both the acquirer and the acquiree, regarding the value drivers, the end-state operating mode, and everybody's roles and responsibilities. Otherwise, there will be confusion and disappointment, and the future will be bleak all around, no matter what the original intentions were.

I recall one acquisition where I was with the acquiring company, and this was clearly an acquisition, not a merger of equals. The companies had previously been competing in the marketplace. To make the acquisition accretive, we were chartered with integrating the acquisition quickly and moving our technology into their sales channel while winding down development of their future products. However, the acquired company was told that they were actually very good at process and operations, that they had the stronger customer relationships, and that they had strong technology. We understood that we had to move fast. They understood that we were going to study the processes, reengineer, and move more slowly and deliberately. We understood that our products were the future; they understood that their products were the future. Our goals were not aligned, so there was no foundation for a successful integration of the two companies to realize the value and returns outlined in the original acquisition business case.

Move quickly. Time is your enemy in mergers and acquisitions (M&A). The faster you move, the better. Realize that you will make mistakes. People will automatically fill whatever available time you give them, so time-box the activities, and as long as the value drivers are well understood, the right activities will be the focus.

Measure everything you can. Measure what works and what doesn't work, and learn from each transaction. This is crucial in successfully navigating a merger or acquisition.

Consider the people. Remember that M&A puts tremendous pressure on an organization, and in the end it is often all about the people. Treat the people whose positions are eliminated with respect; they are future customers. Treat the new employees who join the organization as you would treat a new hire who you have just spent months to recruit. Spend more time on management, communication, and alignment activities, as you have just introduced great change and uncertainty into an otherwise stable ecosystem, and this is the only way to move the organization to a new equilibrium.

Be a professional. If you are going to lose your own job as part of the merger or acquisition, but you are being asked to stay on during the transition, don't pout or slack off or, even worse, try to sabotage the new management team. First, a professional continues doing the job to the best of his or her ability right up until the last day. You are still a highly paid employee; you are now being paid to help during the transition. Second, you don't want to burn any bridges with the new management team. They may be asked to provide references for you. You may even eventually be asked to return to work for the new company. In some cases, the new managers may be so impressed with you that they will change their mind and ask you to stay on board.

Surviving a Layoff

HAVE YOU BEEN laid off recently? Was it a shock? Did you anticipate the layoff but nevertheless it was painful? Are you still numb and feeling down and out from the experience? Was it just you who was laid off, your whole group, or a massive number of people across the board? If you haven't been laid off yet, do you see the writing on the wall, given the decline in your company or industry? How will you deal with the uncertainty and transition? How will you start a job search if you haven't had to look for a job in years? Do you know someone—your spouse, a family member, or a good friend—who is trying to make it through a layoff?

● DEFINING THE CHALLENGE

A layoff is a common problem that won't go away anytime soon. Layoffs are all around us. Organizations of all kinds are rebalancing, restructuring, and reorganizing. Whatever you call it, a layoff means that your job goes away and you need to look for a new one. Most employers provide severance pay and career transition services. Often, however, this is not enough to help you land your next job. You'll need to take charge and own your career more than ever during this challenging time.

Whether the layoffs are massive, impacting hundreds or thousands of people, or smaller in scale, anyone who has been laid off or who is close to someone who has been understands the highly charged emotions that the situation brings. Denial, anger, loss of identity, grief, fear, and hopelessness are all common emotions when you have lost your job.

A layoff can be a challenge, for several reasons. You may not have had to look for a job in a long time and don't know how to conduct a job search. You could have let your network, résumé, and job-search skills become outdated. You may not even be sure what kind of next job you want.

● FACING THE CHALLENGE

In my corporate experience, layoffs were one of the most painful processes that I had to plan and implement. Whether it was one person, 100, or 5,000, what made me feel better about the layoffs was knowing that I could offer some concrete hope and help. Through designing in-company career centers and providing individual career advice for employees, I tried to make everyone's career transition as painless as possible. Happily, I also noted that many not only survived but, rather, thrived through their layoffs. These employees were people with a resilient attitude who took some specific actions to make the best of their situations. More often than not, these folks found even better jobs and more fulfilling work. They moved on successfully and productively.

This chapter offers strategies and tips about surviving your layoff and using it as a fresh start, a new beginning, to something better, bigger, or more fulfilling. Try all or some of the following strategies, tips, and to do's. Choose which will work for you to create a unique solution for yourself. Make sure not to limit yourself to the strategies, tips, and to do's that seem comfortable and within easy reach for you. Take yourself outside your comfort zone. Stretch yourself and go for the ideas that can really change your life or your luck!

An Ending and a Beginning

Let it all out. Give yourself time to process your emotions. Acknowledge them and do what you need to do in order to deal with them productively. Talk with someone who cares. Engage in a physical activity you enjoy, such as golf, running, or a spinning class. Go to the beach and yell at the top of your lungs or build a campfire. Write down your emotions and feelings in your journal.

The point is to let yourself feel your emotions: denial, fear, anger, resentment, anxiety, grief, or whatever. Note that every ending is also a new beginning.

Get by with a little help from your friends. Ask for help or support from your friends or family. If they are not available, seek out an understanding, willing-to-listen colleague, your company's EAP (Employee Assistance Program) counselor, a Human Resources professional, a career transition or outplacement professional, or your minister, rabbi, priest, or spiritual adviser.

Set a target date. Give yourself a time limit for when you'll stop venting about your layoff and start moving on, getting to work on the next career move. It's the sooner the better for you to embrace your fresh start and begin a new chapter in your career.

Making the Adjustment

Know you have options. Remember that you have options. You'll have to put forth the effort to realize them, of course, but they are out there. You could:

- Find another full-time job within your company.
- Go to work for yourself by taking on projects as an independent contractor or consultant.
- Take a break if your severance is generous or you have a nice nest egg or cash reserve, then look for a job.
- Go back to school full-time or part-time, or take a certification program to try something that's always interested you.
- Try out some completely new industries, jobs, or locations as an apprentice, intern, temp, or volunteer, and make a major career change.

Depersonalize the layoff. Don't beat yourself up or play the blame game. In most cases, if you were a poor performer you would have been on corrective action or fired by now. The supply of qualified employees is way too abundant for organizations to keep poor performers or deadwood, so forget laying a guilt trip on yourself. Most likely there was nothing you could have done to stop the layoff. Layoffs are not under your control. Yours was most likely not about your performance. On the flip side, remember that your employer is not a monster. The company did what it had to do for the business's needs—to survive or to improve its performance in challenging times.

Give yourself a happy ending. Say so long to your colleagues. Thank the people who have gone out of their way to help you or with whom you have enjoyed working. Get their contact information and give them your contact information. Ask them to keep in touch and do the same.

Make your lasting connections. For everyone you can't see or talk with before you leave, connect with them by e-mail. Let them know you are leaving and how to stay in touch with you. Hotmail, Yahoo!, and others have free e-mail, so there is no excuse not to open a new e-mail account so that people can stay in touch with you. Use your e-mail to let people know briefly what you think you'll be looking for as a next job. Give them a few ideas on how they can help you. For example, you could ask them to let you know if they have openings in their own companies, know some good executive recruiters, or could suggest leads in particular industries, kinds of jobs, or regions.

Take Advantage of What the Company Offers

Use it; don't lose it. Find out what your employer is offering in terms of career transition or outplacement services and resources. Take full advantage of them. Ask how and when you can use the resources and services and if there are any time limits. Whether there are formal career transition services, an on-site career center, or informal help, make sure to use it all. Normally you would have to pay for this kind of assistance, so consider it a good investment of time. By using these services, you are actually saving money out of your own pocket. Even if you take away only a few insights or helpful tidbits, you actively benefited your career transition.

Ask about kinds of services and resources. Below are common career transition services that organizations offer. If they are not provided to laid-off employees formally, you might be able to talk the company into offering them informally to you or to the group:

- Group workshops on the range of job search skills. These could include self-assessment, résumé writing, interviewing skills, and compensation negotiation.
- Time with an individual career counselor or coach. This person could help you clarify what your interests and possible next moves are; set job search objectives and build an action plan; and guide you to resources or additional help on the tools and resources you'll need, such as referral to a career support group or information on how to break into a specific industry or field.
- Access to an internal job posting board (electronic or hard copy) that lists openings inside the company.
- A compiled list of or links to outside job opportunities.
- Temporary office space and administrative support for conducting your job search. For example, there may be workstations set up with telephones, computers, Internet connections, and administrative support for résumés and photocopying.
- A career center. These are more rare, but some companies, especially the larger or more visionary ones, offer on-site career centers. These provide temporary office space, on-site career advisers, career change and job-search related programs and workshops, and lots of valuable resources.

Ask for a bump up in your package. Figure out if there is a material difference between the career transition services you are offered and the next level up. Sometimes everyone gets the same "package" of career transition and outplacement services. Other times, there may be different levels of benefits for an individual contributor, a manager, a director or vice president, or a senior manager or executive. If you believe the more extensive services are critical to you, try for them. Be prepared to make a strong case for why you deserve the higher level of assistance. Sometimes there is flexibility or a bona fide business rationale for an exception to be granted. For example, perhaps you have been performing the responsibilities of the next higher job because the person was on leave and you just didn't have the title. The company will have to do what's equitable for everyone laid off, but it doesn't hurt to ask for more if you can get it.

Get to Work on Finding Your Next Job

Set up your new office. Your full-time job is now to find a new job, it is hoped a better job, so you must act accordingly. Make a space in your house or apartment for working on your career transition. Set up a nice home office, even if it's a closet, a space on your dining room table, or on the deck in your backyard. Your immediate work will be focused on you—figuring out what you want to do next, making a job search action plan, and implementing it.

Give yourself structure. Your work is now on You, Inc. It's your job to find your next job and to make it as good as it can get. Put yourself on a work schedule. Go to work everyday. Even if you don't feel like it some days, do what you need to get out of bed, get dressed for work, and get going. Create some work structure as you would in your normal job. Wake up at the same time each day. Go through your morning routine. Set clear goals and objectives for what to accomplish that day, that week, and within the next month or so. Make your to-do and project lists. Take lunch or other breaks as you usually would.

Prepare to develop a job search action plan. Look back at Chapter 1 for an in-depth discussion of how to develop an effective job-search action plan. To prepare yourself for that, take a peek at the career management model at the end of this chapter. As homework, answer the three "SAM" questions outlined with the model. Embrace the idea that careers are ever-evolving. People are continuously changing jobs and in motion with their careers.

Stay motivated. Take it one day at a time. Talk to some laid-off colleagues from your organization or others who have landed great jobs. There is comfort in knowing that others made it through their layoffs just fine. Reach out to these people and ask for their advice. Also, don't be shy. Ask if they have job leads, contacts, or offers that they turned down that might still be available.

● Tools and Resources

Reality Check-Up

Do a reality check with yourself to point yourself in the right direction for your career or transition from the get-go. To gain more clarity about what you want to do as a next move, do your self-assessment work first. A vital part of any job search or career change is to reflect and be brutally honest with yourself on the answers to some fundamental questions. Guide yourself through these important questions and determine the dimensions that will help you find out what you are thinking, feeling, and wanting to do at this stage in your career. Your answers will be a valuable foundation for taking the critical next steps in your career:

- *Do I want to try to stay within the company?* This may or may not be an option. Some companies make a genuine effort to fill any openings with laid-off employees before recruiting outside. If it is a possibility to try for another job within your organization, get yourself into the flow of information about where the openings are. Find out whom to speak with and how to interview for the jobs. Sometimes, especially if you have been a strong performer, you may be able informally to create a new job for yourself elsewhere in the company. If there is something valuable you can offer that the company needs, then make a case for it. Talk with someone who can be an advocate for you or who can create a job in his group. Just because the company is laying off in some parts of the organization does not always mean it is not hiring or creating jobs in other areas that are more critical for the company at the time.
- *Who would be helpful in locating or creating a job for me within the company—which colleagues, higher-ups, direct reports, current or*

past managers? Call on support from anyone who can be a champion for you to brainstorm ideas, give you leads, open doors, or lend help to your efforts.

- *If I am leaving the company, how can I use this time—the transition period—as an opportunity to do better? What does "better" look like for me? What does it mean in terms of job content—kinds of responsibilities, compensation and benefits, people I'd like to work with, job titles, schedules, industries, types of organizations, management styles, and locations?*
- *Do I want to stay in the same industry? If not, what are the top two or three industries that I have always dreamed about or been interested in?*
- *Do I want to do the same kind or different work? If I want a change, what are the top two or three functions, fields, or professions that I have always dreamed about or been interested in?*
- *Do I want stay in the same city or move to a different city or country where the job market is better for what I have to offer?*
- *What industry, kinds of organizations, and jobs/fields are preferred and realistic given my financial situation or constraints?*
- *How long can I live on my savings or my reserve? Can I wait until my severance runs out to begin a job search? Will I need to work part-time while in a job search, or do I have a financial cushion to focus full-time on the search for a certain number of months? If I must work part-time, what kind of work can I do so that I maintain schedule flexibility and the energy to focus on my job search?*
- *Can I afford to make a career change now, which will most likely be at a lower salary? How much of a lower-paying job could I take if it means I will be happier or more fulfilled, or that the job will be more stable? What's my baseline salary—how much money must I make to live on?*
- *How long should I give myself to find my next job?* Although the sooner, the better, the average is about one month for every $10,000 you make in salary. In tough job markets, it could take on average two months per every $10,000. For example, a job paying $70,000 could take between seven and fourteen months. If you catch some lucky breaks, are extremely competitive and qualified,

and are trying for an industry or field in which candidates are in more demand, you could land a job in a few weeks or months.

Career Management Model for a Lifetime

Familiarize yourself with the career management model that follows (Figure 16-1). It is a helpful tool to use for a specific job search or a major career change, or to keep referring back to at various stages in your career over your lifetime.

Focus on the center of the circle for now. Look at the bull's-eye on the target: "SAM." Ask yourself three essential questions for your job search ahead:

1. How do I define *success*? Is it money, power, a corner office, being on the A list and moving in the elite social circles, changing the world, building a great product or company, helping people, retir-

Figure 16-1. Lifelong Career Management

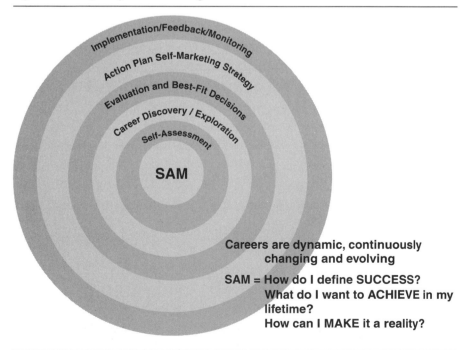

ing by the age of 50, providing financial security to provide a comfortable lifestyle for my loved ones? What is success in my own terms, not others' expectations?

2. What is left that I want to *achieve* in my lifetime? How does my work or career fit into the context of my total life vision?

3. How can I *make* my career goals and objectives a reality in my next job?

Best of the Web

There are more than 2,500 job and career-related Web sites. The following are some of my favorites to give you a sense that there are jobs out there—there's plenty of hope and help. Additional sites are included at the end of Chapter 1.

- America's Job Bank—*www.ajb.dni.us/.* Posts over 1 million jobs that you can search on by job category, zip code, or city. Offers an online personal career center, résumé and cover letter advice, employment and relocation resources, testing and assessment, career tools, and a newsroom.
- Best Job USA—*www.bestjobsusa.com/sections/CAN-careerfairs/index .asp.* Complete list of national career fairs.
- Bloomberg.com—*www.bloomberg.com/careers/* Excellent site for financial jobs for professionals in financial markets, accounting, consulting, management, computer services, telecommunications, marketing, and sales. Job seekers can e-mail résumés directly to employers.
- CareerBuilder—*www.careerbuilder.com.* A comprehensive site with more than 300,000 jobs, a company search function, pointers to employers and ad agencies, résumé advice, relocation services, and a layoff survival kit.
- Careerjournal.com—*www.careerjournal.com.* A great site for executives and senior managers. You get access to regional news, job listings, career advice, negotiation tips, career indicators, and hot career issues. This site allows you to research publicly traded companies that post their jobs with one-click access to the WSJ.com's

Briefing Books. Strategic alliances with Futurestep, Exec-U-Net, Job-Star, FreeAgent.com, and others.

- Craigslist.org—*www.craigslist.org.* Started out in the San Francisco-San Jose Bay Area as a grassroots community of sharing job postings and information. Excellent job postings for both small and large companies, a helpful message board, and news site. Other local area sites included hyperlinked as well.

- Flipdog.com—*www.flipdog.com.* Offers a career center and resources such as advice, newsletters, and job searching 24/7. Permits you to research thousands of employers based on your search criteria. It includes a neat feature for jobs around the world, such as a figure painter in Great Britain, writers in Russia, or a nanny in Australia.

- Guru.com—*www.guru.com.* Look for contract, part-time, and consulting jobs.

- Hot Jobs—*www.hotjobs.com.* HotJobs.com is designed to deliver fast, direct access to quality jobs at the world's top companies to experienced professionals across industries.

- QSnetwork.com—*www.qsnetwork.com.* An international network for careers and top universities worldwide. Provides specialized Web sites and resources for graduates, MBAs, and others to link with executive communities, recruiters, and universities.

Making a Major Career Change

ARE YOU READY for a big career change? Are you not sure where you'll end up but you know you have to make a move from what you are doing now? Have you been unhappy in your career for a while—unmotivated, bored, or not stimulated—and you need a change? Do you feel burned out, with nothing left to give? Is the work you are doing intense and all-consuming, leaving little time for family or outside interests? Do you want your life back or at least a career where there is more work-life balance? Are you one of the lucky ones who has achieved your financial goals and now you have the freedom to pursue your dream job, your passion? Do you have a wonderful spouse or partner who can support your family financially while you go for what you've always wanted to do?

A major career change could be going from high technology to opening a doggie daycare and training facility; from banking to body work (massage therapy and Rolfing); from Human Resources professional to fashion stylist; from working with an airline to opening a bed-and-breakfast inn; from strategy consulting to working in a nonprofit organization.

● DEFINING THE CHALLENGE

For our purposes, we define a major career change as a new job function, field, or profession. For example, you change from a marketing job function to finance or from operations to strategic planning. You are in the health-care field and want to try something in entertainment or move from venture capital into sports management. You may be a doctor by profession and desire a change to a biotechnology start-up company, or to being a financial adviser, portfolio manager, or consultant to corporations developing employee health and fitness programs.

Making a major change to a new (destination) career can be both daunting and difficult. For starters, you have already invested a great deal of time and energy in your current career. You will have to leave most of that behind to start all over again. You will have to reestablish yourself and rebuild a track record. Most probably, you will also have to take salary reduction. Although you may have transferable education and experience, you may not have the specific experience in the new function, field, or profession. For employers, it doesn't matter what salary you were making before. They will pay you for what you can do for or contribute to the new job. That means less than you are making now until you gain more experience and show results in your new career.

Making a major career change also means that you will be competing for jobs with an oversupply of qualified candidates who are out of work and eager to take a job even several levels below what their backgrounds warrant. Although some fields are growing so fast that there are more jobs than candidates (a seller's market), this is usually the exception. Your job search in a new field will usually take double the effort than if you were staying in the same career. Repositioning your résumé, gaining some relevant experience, networking into the destination career, and other key steps will take time and know-how. If this is not enough to dissuade you, you also should know that many of your friends and family will think you are crazy—especially if you are great at what you do and make a good living. Those close to you may think you have a screw loose if you want to give it all up to make a major career change.

● FACING THE CHALLENGE

This may seem like a bleak picture. There certainly are hurdles when you make a major career change. Indeed, making a major career change is not for the timid or undetermined. You will need the diligence of an athlete. You need to gear up for a marathon, not a sprint. For those of you who are toying with the idea of jumping that hurdle or are in the throes of doing so, you know the amount of mental, physical, emotional, and spiritual preparation you need. There are also the factors of luck, timing, and support from those who believe in you and will take the time to coach you or to cheer you on from the sidelines until you cross the finish line.

Making a major career change can bring numerous positives. These include:

- A more satisfying and meaningful work life
- Potential for higher compensation in the future
- A boost of career or professional growth
- Fresh intellectual stimulation
- A new sense of accomplishment
- A fresh start to do something you truly love or totally enjoy

In this chapter, you will learn how you can make a major career change as effectively and quickly as possible. Use the strategies and tips that follow in conjunction with those in Chapters 2, 3, and 4 for a maximum-strength solution.

Before you start to work on making your major career change, though, you will need to do your homework. As a strong foundation, you will need to clarify your purpose, your passion, and path. Take a look at Chapter 21 and use the exercises, tools, and resources at the end of the chapter. You will need to research industries and functions, fields, and professions to determine what you are interested in. Review Chapter 1 for guidance on this; this chapter picks up where that work has left off.

Do You Know Where You're Going?

Be clear about your destination career. Where is it that you want to go? Describe it. Flesh it out. Give it shape, dimension, and life. Here are some examples to get your wheels turning:

- Steve Fraiser is an investment banker who wants to do something related to his great passion and talent for golf. A friend of a friend is a structural engineer who, in his spare time, has designed an innovative line of golf clubs. He now wants to make a go of selling the clubs and starting a viable business. Steve could join him to make the clubs a viable product, market them, and get financing to start a business. Another option for Steve is to become a golf pro at the new luxury hotel and golf course in town. Or maybe he will teach golf on a few cruises or through the local community college or at a private high school to gain experience in his destination career.

- Halle Baylor is an English teacher who desires a change to writing screenplays and ultimately to directing films. Since childhood, a favorite "craft" of hers has been storytelling. As young as age eight, Halle wrote plays and organized the neighborhood children to perform them. With her ever-present video camera, she made films in her backyard and later on in college; she acted or worked behind the scenes in many theater productions. Halle makes a move to Los Angeles and through a colleague, a drama teacher, lands a job as a personal assistant on a small-budget movie. She works her way up to reading scripts. She prepares to audition for *Project Green Light,* a reality show designed to find, mentor, and finance new directing and screenwriting talent, established by Matt Damon and Ben Affleck. She actively meets people in the entertainment industry and starts to build connections.

Leverage your strengths and experience. Remember that there is a significant difference between what you are good to great in and what you actually want to do and use in your destination career. For example, maybe you are an awesome manager of people, but in your new career you would prefer not to take on that responsibility. You'd like to be more of an individual contributor so that you can focus on the content of your work and have more time for your interests outside of work, too. Perhaps your ability with numbers and analytics is exceptional but in your new career, you really want to use your artistic and creative talents on a daily basis.

Ask yourself what strengths and experience you want to use predominantly in your destination career. If you are considering among multiple new career directions, which one or two of these are the best fits with the strengths and experience you want to leverage.

Preparing to Market Yourself

Reposition yourself. Refer to the marketing 5 P's in Chapter 1. Think about yourself as a product, a "brand" or a company (You, Inc.). Focus particularly on how you will position yourself to potential employers vis-à-vis others vying for the available jobs. Identify your tangible and compelling transferable experience, strengths, and skills. In other words, what have you done in your past work and which strengths and skills are relevant to the change you wish to make? Which of these can translate to your new career? How do you convey that to the potential employers? If you choose to work for yourself, how do you convey your experience, strengths, and skills to your potential clients?

Determine what you are willing to sacrifice. Get your finances in order to accommodate a pay cut for a while. Do your homework on what is realistic compensation in the new function, field, or profession. What do people make starting out? How about five years into the career? What do top executives make (if that is something you aspire to)?

Think long and hard about the sacrifices. Is the change truly one that you are willing and able to live with? In addition to the finances, think about what other sacrifices, adjustments, or trade-offs you will need to make. Will there be downgrades in status, in benefits (title, health insurance, gym memberships, company car, or number of vacation days)? Is the career change worth the trade-off to you? Perhaps you will have to give up aspects of your current career that you enjoy and appreciate, such as great colleagues, a wonderful boss, job security, or prestige. Are you okay with letting these go for the potential of attaining your destination career?

Get real. When you are trying to make your crossover to the new career, you will experience doubts, frustrations, and setbacks. You need to anchor yourself with the resolve that you are choosing to make the change. You want to do it and you will make it to the finish line. Walk, run, crawl, or be carried when you are your weariest, but keep the faith.

Launching Your Career Change

Use your school's alumni career services. Your school's career services for alumni are a great resource for a job search or a career change. Typically your undergraduate and graduate programs offer career services for alumni. Check out the school's Web site or call the school's general number and ask for Alumni Relations or the Career Services or Career Management Center. Speak with the director or someone in charge of alumni career services to get an overview of what they provide. Ask specifically about help with making a major career change. Many schools offer over-the-telephone career counseling. They host career networking events and workshops in cities around the country, even worldwide. Find out if there is an alumni directory—a list of all alumni categorized by industry, job function, and/or geographic location. This list could be in printed format or, better yet, in a searchable database format. Alumni are a fantastic network to call on.

Make contact. Select a short list of alumni you will contact based on those closest to or already in your destination career. Conduct an informational interview (refer to Chapter 4 for guidelines and sample questions). Ask these alumni contacts for advice on breaking into the new industry or obtaining the new kind of job. Ask for their perspectives on which companies are the best to work for and which ones are hiring. Ask if they can refer you to people in the industry who may have job openings in their own organizations. If you really connect with someone you contact, ask if the person will advise you periodically or act as an informal mentor as you are trying to make your career change.

Sign up for a course. Try a low-risk, low-cost, career exploration or career development course at your local community college. These are good investments to help you gain clarity on your new career. These courses typically last 8 to 12 weeks and include self-assessment exercises, helpful reading and discussion, and guest speakers from different industries or fields.

Start your own career change action group. Invite 7 to 10 people who are in job searches and career transitions to meet regularly. Trade off hosting each meeting. Share tips, leads, contacts, and support. If you want to go the whole ten yards, invite different guest experts or people who have recently made major career changes. They can share valuable perspectives, insights, and advice. *Note*: A side benefit of starting a career action group is that each person in the group is leaving one career and making a move to another. That means that the person leaving a career can also serve as an expert for others who may want to move into that career.

Recruit a recruiter. If the destination career is one that relies heavily on executive recruiters for hiring mid- to senior-level managers—that is, about $80,000 annual compensation plus—enlist the help of an executive recruiter from the function, field, or profession. Well-known, elite firms such as Korn Ferry International, Russell Reynolds, Spencer Stuart, and Egon Zhender handle CEO, executive team, vice president, and director-level roles for organizations from Fortune 500 companies to venture capital backed start-ups. Small boutique firms or one-person shops may handle searches with compensation levels as low as $50,000.

Enlisting a recruiter is a difficult feat, but if you can finesse it, the benefits are invaluable. Typically, you don't call recruiters; they call you. They are extremely busy and usually engage themselves only for clients who are retaining them (read: paying them) to search for candidates for specific openings. In working a lot with these professionals during my corporate days when recruiting executives, I came to appreciate the natural gift they have for helping people realize their career potential and for matching employers with great people for their jobs.

If you can somehow connect with a recruiter, he or she can provide quick, potent help for your career change. In 15 or 20 minutes, what a recruiter can tell you is priceless. Some specific questions to ask a recruiter are:

- Who are the key players or employers in your destination career?
- Which companies are hiring, which are not?
- Who are the up-and-comers on the brink of being the next big thing?
- What is the ideal profile or candidate background required for the kinds of roles or jobs you are interested in?
- Which companies hire from the outside and are more flexible in accepting nontraditional backgrounds?
- What are the compensation levels and possible career paths for the industries or jobs you are seeking?
- Assess your background; how marketable are you?

- Do you realistically have a shot at making this career change? If yes or maybe, what can you do to be a stronger contender? If no, why?
- What advice does he or she have for breaking into the industry or successfully making the career change?

Finding a Mentor

Getting hired as an apprentice is an excellent way to gain experience for your destination career; you learn from someone experienced in your desired new field or industry. Be creative and resourceful to identify a list of possible mentors. Ideally, your wish list would include experts—renowned and respected in the field—and/or those who don't have fancy titles or familiar names but would be great mentors or teachers.

There is a lot of advice to give about trying to get hired as an apprentice. Achieving this is complicated, can take a long time, and is admittedly a long shot. It's worth a full discussion, however, because if you are lucky and tenacious enough to land an apprenticeship, the rewards are numerous:

- You gain first-hand experience and knowledge about what it takes to succeed in your destination career and learn the ins and outs of the business.
- Your mentor could create an actual job for you because you become indispensable.
- He or she could give you access or referrals to a circle of friends and business contacts, opening the door wide for you.
- Your mentor could serve as a valuable reference and vouch for your potential.
- The time with your mentor is both an important rite of passage and credible work experience to others in the field or industry for when you start to interview for jobs.

A mentor can be a man or a woman, old, middle-aged, or even young. The individual can have a CEO or high-level title or no title at all. The person may work for him or herself or do freelance consulting. An apprenticeship can last a few days, a few weeks, months, or longer, depending on what you can work out. Starting with a short amount of time, like a few weeks, is usually better because you can always extend it if the situation is working out.

How to Get Hired as an Apprentice

Let's use an example first so you get the basic idea, then review some creative ways for getting hired as an apprentice. Suppose you want to make a major career change into real estate. You just bought a new home from the grand dame of real estate in your area. Her name is Sally. You and your husband had a pleasant experience and made a nice connection with her.

Make contact. Call Sally. Let her know you are thinking of a career change to her field and want to learn from the very best. Tell her you'd appreciate her ideas and advice. Invite Sally for coffee or lunch or ask her to drop by to see what you've done to your new home. When you get together, be ready to make some engaging small talk, then ask your questions. Convey that you know you have a lot to learn and that you are eager to learn from the best!

Pursue the relationship in a natural way. At the end of your time together, ask Sally for another meeting. Try for something that she would enjoy. For example, if you know she is an avid walker, invite her to walk along one of her favorite trails. If she likes arts and wine, ask her to go with you to an upcoming Arts and Wine Festival or to view the new exhibit at the Museum of Modern Art. Do what you can to build the relationship as naturally as possible.

Try for an apprenticeship. At some point, when you have established a good rapport, ask Sally if you can watch her in action. Suggest that she let you "shadow" her around for a week, a month, or so. This means you tag along or listen in on what Sally does in her typical work day. Unobtrusively, you get to see what her day-to-day activities are. This kind of first-hand experience will be invaluable. You can learn the ins and outs of the business and see what it takes for someone to succeed in your destination career.

Learn all you can. Getting hired as an apprentice means that you will try to soak up everything like a sponge: your mentor's knowledge; how to interact with her clients, staff, or others; the actual responsibilities and duties of the business; what it's like to walk in her shoes. Apprenticing also means that you pitch in to help when you can so that you are learning about and handling the ropes from the ground up.

Get involved. Ask your mentor if there are projects or activities that you could help with. Better yet, identify where you can assist based on your observations and active listening. During your time with your mentor, look out for problems—something that's not working as well as it could or specific responsibilities that your mentor doesn't like to do or gets frustrated about. If you have the skills or abilities or knowledge to help out or fix it, jump in with both feet. Offer to help however you can to ease the workload.

For example, if the receptionist called in sick and the telephones are ringing off the hook, volunteer to fill in. You'll learn a lot from hearing what the people who call are saying. Or let's say your mentor has been engaged by a company that is moving its corporate headquarters and thousands of employees to the area, to consult on the relocation, home buying, and so on. Your mentor has to make a presentation to the Human Resources group that evening and has not had time to develop the PowerPoint slides, a customized report about homes currently available with certain specifications, and handouts. You can offer to do it and to accompany her to the meeting. You may need a few minutes of the mentor's time to give you ideas on where to get the information and any other suggestions, but you can then take the ball and run with it.

This is one example of how someone can get hired as an apprentice and leverage the experience to the fullest. You get the gist. It is hoped that this experience will be food for thought. Once you get hired as an apprentice, view everything as a learning experience useful in judging whether the field is for you or not. If it is, you'll have a strong base for your launch pad. The experience can also be called out on your résumé and in your future interviewing. You will have picked up some new valuable skills, experience, and knowledge along the way. The time learning with your mentor will help get you started in your new career.

Approaching a Mentor You Don't Know

If you want to apprentice but don't know the person you are approaching, you will have to do a little extra homework and try harder. It will be like a sales cold call. Since the person has no connection to you, there is high likelihood he will say no to whatever you ask. You will need to be tenacious, creative, and resourceful.

First, figure out a way to get an audience with the person you'd like to apprentice with. You need to open the door. Ask around in your circle of friends and business contacts to see if anyone can make a referral or give you ideas on how best to approach your prospect. Learn all you can about his background and figure out clever ways you may be able to meet. Try to find out through a Google or Yahoo! search, reviewing the company's Web site, and reading articles about the mentor. Glean all you can about:

- What motivates your mentor
- What inspired him to get into the field or business
- What his accomplishments and failures are
- What his management and lifestyle are—how does your mentor seem to do business and live life?
- His education, family, favorite charities or causes, outside interests such as a love for golf, the New York Yankees, sailing, the ballet, or old convertible cars

Each situation will be different, but here are some ideas that have worked for others:

- Try to interview your potential mentor for a story you will write for your alumni magazine, a newsletter you contribute to, or the like.
- Volunteer with her favorite charity and at some point, you may be able to ask for an introduction or make a point of being at an event or meeting together.
- Be direct and write a letter or follow up with a telephone call. Tell why you admire the mentor and why you'd like to meet with her.
- Ask a favor of a friend who has an in with one of your prospective mentor's outside interests and somehow create an intriguing invitation or interaction that will include your being there, too.
- Place yourself in her orbit and see if you get lucky. Where might she get a cup of coffee, go out for drinks or lunch, walk the family dogs, buy groceries, go for a haircut, or go for a jog?

- Network in through her spouse or partner. If your prospective mentor is married, find out about the spouse's work, community involvement, or interests. For example, maybe the family has set up a foundation and your prospective mentor's spouse is the head of it. Maybe you learn in passing that you went to the same high school, are from the same town, or both frequent a favorite bookstore or vintage clothing store. Figure out how you can connect, build a rapport, and take it from there.

Some Words of Caution

Use your common sense. What we are talking about is being creative, resourceful, and within bounds—pushing the envelope to make your own luck. It is about trying to find a way to meet your prospective mentor and get hired as an apprentice. We are not talking about being in-your-face, pushy, overaggressive, or going outside the bounds of respect and decency. You won't hide in the bushes outside the mentor's home, but you may run into the person at a favorite restaurant and go over to introduce yourself briefly. You won't volunteer with a pet charity just to meet, then quit as soon as you've introduced yourself. You will contribute real time and effort to the charity, with the side hope and possible benefit of meeting the individual.

Know what you're going to say. When you do meet your prospective mentor, have your two-minute elevator pitch ready. You know—if you were in the elevator with a CEO or someone important and wanted to make a positive impression, what would you say? Create your "opening." Then once you have connected with the person, take it from there to cultivate a rapport that can lead to your apprenticing.

Tell the truth. Be honest about wanting a career change, wanting to learn and benefit from his knowledge and experience. Be compelling and genuine about why. Tell him you want to learn from the best and are willing to work hard. Let your mentor know what you have to offer to make it in the field. Engage the individual and ask thoughtful questions, such as:

- "How did you get started in the business?"
- "What inspires and motivates you?"
- "What are your most pressing challenges and priorities?"
- "What regrets, if any, do you have about your career?"
- "Where and how can you use extra help?"
- "Would you be open to spending a few days with me shadowing you so I can see you in action, like a day on the job?"

Make yourself valuable. If you are fortunate enough to get a day or few days with the mentor—for example, a mini-apprenticeship—then you can try to extend your time, keep on learning, and make yourself indispensable. Based on your active listening, look for the links between what's important or of interest to your teacher and what you can offer from your portfolio of strengths, skills, and abilities. Suggest some concrete ways you can contribute to his business and priorities while you are also learning on the job. Be bold. Be audacious.

Don't expect compensation. As an apprentice you will have to work for free, but if you become indispensable or do such a bang-up job, who knows—maybe your mentor will create a role for you. At minimum, she will serve as an important reference and may offer you access to valuable contacts, opening the door for your career change. You will also gain the insider's view on how the business or field works and what it takes to be successful.

Give something back. Being an apprentice is as reciprocal as you can make it. It's about giving and receiving as much as possible. It's not about a one-sided relationship. You try to give something back in return for your valuable learning experience—if not during the time you are apprenticing, then later on when you are in a position to do so. You might not ever be able to match the value of what the apprenticeship gives to you, but you can give whatever you are able. This may mean sending some clients his way, writing a letter of recommendation for his son or daughter to your alma mater, building a custom bike or set of golf clubs if that's your hobby, or sending him and his wife the best bottle of champagne when you get your first job in your new career.

Doing Volunteer or Temp Work

Volunteer for the industry or professional association. Get involved in the destination career's professional association. Volunteer to serve on the committee of organizers for the annual conference, edit or graphic-design the newsletter, even offer to take photos at the events or help maintain the Web site. Do what you can to get your foot firmly in the door. Often, it doesn't matter how old or young you are or what industry you are coming from. Associations generally need people and resources.

Professional associations offer benefits like internship opportunities, continuing education programs for keeping abreast of the field, workshops for those new to the profession, and a newsletter that includes job postings. Volunteering your time is helpful for networking, getting up to speed on what opportunities are available, and learning about the key players/employers and people in the field.

Try temp or project work. A great way to make a major career change, and to make some money while you are at is, is to do some temp or project work. You'll be able to test-drive your desired change and see what you like, don't like, and want to pursue. Do what you are qualified to do in the organization. Try for something related to your destination career, but be willing to take what you can get and springboard from there. Perform well, get to know as many people as possible, keep your ears open about opportunities (posted or not), and continue opening doors for yourself.

Check out Web sites such as guru.com, freeagent.com, and craigslist .com or find work through an agency such as Robert Half International or M2 Management Maximizers. Take a look at the list of Web sites at the end of Chapter 1. Many of those sites have sections for part-time or temporary and project work.

● TOOLS AND RESOURCES

Repositioning Your Résumé

Since a résumé is like a calling card, a common quick way someone can understand your background, you need to make sure your résumé will be interesting for your destination career. Because you are making a major career change, your résumé will have to compellingly convey to the reviewer your translatable, relevant, transferable skills, abilities, and knowledge. In other words, what your background is and what you have to offer that is directly or indirectly related to your destination career.

Use a functional résumé. A functional résumé highlights your core portfolio of strengths, relevant work experiences, and skills. Determine three to five strengths, skills, or representative work experience that you used in all of your jobs. What were the common ones and which are most valuable to your new career? Use ones that are most applicable to the new jobs or career that you are trying for. For example, suppose you are applying for marketing jobs and in the past you worked as a financial analyst, a golf caddy, and a retail clerk in a computer store. You might use skill headings: Customer Knowledge and Service; P and L/ Financial Analysis Experience; Initiative and Creativity; and Computer Skills. Then under each heading, list PAR achievement statements from any of your jobs that underscore that you have the strength or skill or kind of experience. Take a look at Chapter 3 on strengthening your résumé for an in-depth discussion of a functional résumé.

Develop a positioning statement. When you are changing careers, it is a good idea to use a two- or three-sentence statement about yourself after your identification section. Usually this is centered so it stands out from the rest of your content. The purpose is to establish your positioning with the person reviewing your résumé. This sets the tone and gives a theme to what he or she will read on your résumé.

For example, suppose you have been in venture capital your whole career but want to make a move to an operational role in a high-tech company. You might say:

> "Evaluated and invested in early phase technology companies. Interacted with executive teams, advised on business plans, targets, and building management teams. Gained knowledge of day-to-day operations as board member for several portfolio companies. Can translate strategy to action. Strong implementation skills and know-how to analyze what is not working."

Matching Yourself to a Job's Requirements

Try this exercise using the worksheet in Figure 17-1 to help you. Cut out or print out two or three job ads or postings that you are interested in. Highlight the key requirements. List what the specifications are for: (1) work experience, (2) skills and abilities, (3) education or specialized knowledge, (4) personal qualities, and (5) other (e.g., willing to relocate).

Next to each requirement, note what you have to offer in that category. This will serve as a good base for relaying your relevant and transferable background when applying for the jobs. Draw from your sum total of experiences, skills, abilities, knowledge, and strengths. These include paid or unpaid work, volunteer projects, your hobbies, interests, and educational accomplishments.

Figure 17-1. What a Job Wants—Translate Destination Career Requirements What You Have to What They Want

Employer Qualifications	Destination Career Requirements	What I Have to Offer
Work Experience		
Skills and Abilities		
Education or Specialized Knowledge		
Personal Qualities		
Other		

Taking a Career Break

ARE YOU AT THE TOP of your game but you want to opt out? Perhaps your heart is just not in your work anymore or you've lost your motivation. Have you just completed a long-running, intense project and are ready to get your life back? Have you been a star performer, burning the candle at both ends, and you need some time to replenish? Are the 14-hour days finally getting to you? You aren't able to see your kids grow up or maybe you just want to be able to have dinner at home with your honey more often. Have you had an epiphany that has led you to want to make some drastic changes in your life? Your job or career is at the top of that. Has a friend or loved one died in the last year and you are taking stock of your life and what you want it to look like? Have you been considering time off and then a career change for a while but need some time to think about what you want to do?

If any of these situations sound familiar, it's because they happen to the best among us. Put simply, you have reached a point where you want to or need to take a break.

● DEFINING THE CHALLENGE

All of us who work can use strategic breaks over the lifetime of our careers to transform our work and our lives. Breaks are great to recharge batteries; redirect a career path; reenergize the mind, body, or spirit; regain motivation; or retool with new skills, education, or experiences to advance or completely change a career direction. Taking time off isn't a new concept.

People have been taking breaks—a few months to a few years or more—from their careers for a long time. While there are definitely positives to these breaks, they can be risky and potentially prove to be career-limiting. The reentry into the workforce can be much more difficult than need be if you don't plan the break thoughtfully. You'll also need a reentry strategy.

People take breaks for a variety of reasons. Sometimes the breaks are planned. For example, professors on sabbaticals and actors on hiatus have planned career breaks. Professionals in high-intensity careers such as entrepreneurs, investment banking, venture capitalists, or management consulting may step out, take extended time off, and then jump back into their next work venture.

Breaks may also be unplanned. A layoff, juggling career and family such as having a baby or caring for a sick parent, and trailing a partner or spouse to a new location are examples of when someone might be forced to take a career break.

There are four common problems associated with taking a career break and coming back from it:

1. You may not know how to do it with the least risk and disruption to your career.

2. Your skills and experience could become obsolete while you're on your break.

3. You may face a stigma when you want to return to work from managers who view you as unmotivated or "crazy" for leaving such a great job when you did.

4. Even if your break worked wonders for you, reentry into the workforce when you want to can be a problem, especially if you are changing careers.

● FACING THE CHALLENGE

In the big picture of your long-term work life, taking career breaks, whether short or long ones, can be a strategic tool for managing your career actively and keeping it stimulating, interesting, and meaningful. If you can handle the problems that may arise, taking a break can be a powerful impetus for sustaining yourself and your career over a lifetime.

Try all or some of the following strategies, tips, and to-do's. Create a unique solution set for yourself and use what will work best for you. Make sure not only to try the ones that seem comfortable and within reach but to take yourself outside your comfort zone.

Preparing for a Break

Clarify the purpose of your break. Why do you want or need to take time off? For example, do you want to take time off from a dead-end job and figure out what you need to do to change careers? Do you need time off because you have been burning both ends of the candle and must recharge your batteries before you're completely depleted? Do you want to take a career break because you are at a good place financially but not getting any younger? Do you know that what you are doing now is not satisfying and you want something more? Do you have to take a break because you want to care for your terminally ill father or mother? A useful exercise for clarifying the purpose of your break is provided in the last section of this chapter.

Planning Your Break

Think about whether you want to return to your current employer. Whether you plan your break or it is unanticipated, do as much as possible to manage it. If you know you want to take a break, do as much as you can beforehand to ensure the smoothest transition for your employer and yourself. Your reputation is precious and how you treat the situation when you leave a job is just as important as when you start one. If you think you will want to return to your same employer, even if in a different group, talk with your manager and Human Resources to find out what your options are. A mentor in your organization who is well respected can be a good sounding board and give you some guidance before you have these discussions.

Ask for a leave of absence. Large organizations or very progressive ones often have a formal leave of absence policy. Leaves are approved based on business needs, meaning if the business can sustain the person leaving his or her job for an agreed-on amount of time. Formal leaves are typically granted for reasons such as educational purposes (you return to graduate school) or family leave for a new baby or sick parent. These allow for up to 12 months away with a commitment that you return to your same job or one similar. The kinds of leaves we are discussing are more out of the norm. If you want to return to your company, you'll most likely need to fashion something as an informal leave or "sabbatical." Other alternatives are to resign, leaving the door open to return, or to resign, take stock of where you are in your work and life and what you want, and go with wherever that leads you.

Setting up an informal leave of absence. If you think you want to return to your employer, forging an informal leave will require some finesse on your part. If you have built a strong track record of performance and good relationships, you should be able to initiate a leave. Discuss it with your manager and Human Resources, your mentor, or the highest level person possible who would be empathetic. Convey your case with poignant reasons you need to take time off. Be specific within a range of a few months about the amount of time you'd ideally like off. Try to suggest how your work can be transitioned—who can do it and how it can be handled while you are away. Offer to be on call for emergencies, but be careful not to overcommit. Make a "handshake" agreement that the door is open for your return to your same job, if the company can carry on without you while you are away, or one like it. The latter option is possible if there are frequent openings at your level that could use your experience or if the company has the flexibility to create a job for you.

Leaving Your Company

Formulate a communication strategy. Think about these questions. "What will I tell people about my break?" "How will I position it?" "Whom do I need to or want to tell?" "How will I communicate?" Core groups of people you'll want to share your news with include your manager, senior managers who have been supportive of you, your colleagues inside and outside your organization, your staff, vendors, strategic partners, and so on.

Design your communication plan. Take the time to make your communication personalized, not one-size-fits-all. For some, you may meet in person. For others, you may call them or send an e-mail or note. A broadcast e-mail or just including the information in a holiday newsletter may be appropriate for some. A classy, professional communication will convey these points:

- Let people know that you are taking some time off beginning X date.
- Give a short reason why.
- Add something more personal about what you might be doing on your break if appropriate—for example, going back to school, spending some time with your kids before they're off to college, training for a marathon.
- Tell how to contact you while you are off.
- Express how much they've meant to you.

Use your communication to network. If you are not planning to return to your company and know you'll try for a career or company change later on, letting people know about your break is an excellent networking tool. You can put yourself on their radar screens, letting them know you're thinking about a career change or hoping they'll keep you in mind for certain kinds of opportunities. A nice side benefit to communicating with people about your break is that it reduces speculation about the "real reason" you're gone or people's hearing about it via the grapevine. In the absence of information, it's often human nature to think the worst happened—for example, you were fired or asked to leave, had a falling out with the CEO, were really unhappy in some way, and the like.

Give closure to yourself and colleagues. Your employer and/or your colleagues may have traditional ways of saying goodbye to someone who is leaving. Participate in this "ritual," whether it's a lunch, cocktails after work, or a potluck in the conference room. If there is nothing planned for you, throw a party for yourself. Invite as many people as you're comfortable with to your own bon voyage. This allows you to say farewell to as many people as possible in one fell swoop and sends you off on a positive, celebratory note, which it is. Every ending is also a new beginning!

Make a smooth transition. Leave a positive impression of yourself and how you exit the organization. Offer to be involved with the hiring of and/

or transitioning your work to a successor, whether you'll be replaced with someone in your group or a new hire. Make sure to live up to your commitments. Complete all of the projects you are currently working on. Continue to handle your day-to-day responsibilities well until the day you leave. Organize your files and make it easy for someone to step into your job. Offer to let your manager or group call you if they have questions or need emergency help. If you are leaving the company in a lurch by departing suddenly, offer to consult (on an hourly rate) for a set time until a replacement can be found.

Managing Your Break

Address your worst fears head-on. Either as you are planning your break or shortly after you are on it, take the time to address your worst fears about taking the time: the worst-case scenarios and how you might handle them. In doing so, you get them out of the way so you can relax and embrace your break fully. Usually, addressing your worst fears about taking and/or coming back from a break will give you comfort and confidence. You realize that the worst usually is not as bad as it seems. Most things you will be able to handle or do something about.

Others before you have taken breaks and come back from them successfully. Most times, they return to work with renewed vigor and momentum. Also, you can see that whatever your worst fears, there is a lot you can do, manage, and prepare for to ensure that the worst doesn't actually happen. For example, you might fear that your skills will become obsolete. There are steps you can take while you're on break to make sure that your skills are used and continue to develop.

Chill out. Give yourself time to wind down. Take at least a few weeks to relax, play, and engage in what makes you happy, fulfilled, and alive. This may mean spending time with family or friends, reading the stack of books on your bedside table, cooking a healthy dinner every night and enjoying it, catching up on sleep or movies, going on a vacation, fixing things around the house with the DIY projects you've had on hold, or getting back into exercise—whatever works for you.

Get excited about your break. Don't feel guilty or look back. Embrace your break with energy. Use your break to recharge your batteries. This might mean doing volunteer work, getting certified in Pilates, hiking the Grand Canyon, or indulging your love for painting. Redirect a career path. This could mean getting onto or off of the fast track or returning to a field you had moved away from. Reenergize your body and soul. This might mean that you spend your break with friends and family, lend your time and talents to a cause dear to you like sustaining the environment, a political campaign, or world hunger programs. What makes you excited to get out of bed in the mornings to do? Seek out projects, volunteer work, internships, and social activities that allow you the chance to experience what motivates and moves you.

Improve yourself. Develop new skills or go back to school to advance or change a career direction. You may sign up for a full-fledged program like a Masters in Business Administration (MBA) or a certification course such as in Pilates, massage therapy, marriage and family counseling, or network engineering. Other possibilities are specialized training as a real estate agent, pastry chef, or dog trainer through the Humane Society.

Try some short courses. If a formal program is not for you, dabble in a few classes. Try some e-learning, online courses, or DIY. Create informal ways you can get more of the experience and skills you want to build. Informational interview (see Chapter 4) your way to creating an internship, apprenticeship, or work as a "chief of staff" shadowing and assisting someone in his or her job. Learn from a mentor in the new field you are targeting. Volunteer for a project for a nonprofit in the function you may have talent in but not formalized experience. If you have a lot of experience, suggest to the CEO that you will serve as an informal adviser on the most pressing challenges, such as strategy, fund-raising, branding, a capital campaign, or rebounding from a reputational disaster.

For example, perhaps you desire a transition from marketing to finance. Look for a nonprofit that would appreciate your helping them with operating budgets, forecasting, and fund-raising targets. You will gain some valuable finance experience without formally having done that in your past. Perhaps you want to move from strategic planning to pursue your love for restoring old houses. Talk to your friend who is a successful real estate agent, art buyer, and home designer. See if you can apprentice with him for a while to test-drive the profession.

Maintaining Career Fitness

Keep up your strengths and skills. Focus on the key skills and strengths you'll need for your return to the workforce. Do what you can over your break to use these and continue to develop them. Especially in industries or professions that are fast-paced, highly technical, or require constant re-education, you can become a dinosaur pretty quickly. If you plan to make a career change (industry, new function, and/or new organization), identify the core skills and strengths that will make you competitive in order to make that change. Ways to maintain or develop your skills and strengths while you're on break are listed at the end of this chapter.

Sustain key relationships. Figure out which relationships are key to you and make efforts to nurture those, focusing on three to five. Which are key will depend on your situation. It is those people who can help you, be of influence, or provide guidance during or coming back from your break. If you are returning to your company, it may be your boss, the head of HR, or a close colleague who is well regarded and in-the-know. If you are trying for a career change or not sure what you'll do, it may be your boss (remember you'll need a recommendation), a former boss you've lost touch with, and a few well-connected friends who could help you get into your anticipated new industry or field.

Expand your circle of friends. During a break is a perfect time to broaden your circle of friends and career contacts. This doesn't have to be daunting or a lot of extra work. Just be open to new people as you are on your break. Make a point of getting to know someone new at least once a week while doing whatever you're doing or experiencing in your volunteer project, class, fun activities, or your time with friends and family.

Reentering the Workforce

Develop a reentry strategy and plan. Figure that for every $10,000 you want to make in salary, you'll need one month of a job search. For example, if you left your last job making $90,000 and you hope to make between $80,000 and $100,000 in your next job, give yourself between eight and ten months for your search. How much time you need will depend on personal factors such as how clear you are on your purpose, passion, and path; which industries and kinds of jobs and organizations you'll target; and the status of your network, job leads, résumé, and interviewing skills. External factors also can impact how long you'll need for your job search. These include how hot or cold the job market is, the supply of talent for the jobs you'll compete for, and how open your targeted industries or companies are to considering people with transferable but not exact experience, if you are going for a career change.

If you are changing careers after your break, take a look at Chapter 17 on making a major career change. Also review Chapters 1, 3, and 4 on doing a job search, creating a better résumé, and improving your interviewing skills.

● TOOLS AND RESOURCES

Clarifying the Purpose of Your Break

Try this useful and quick exercise. Answer with what comes off the top of your mind. Record or write down your answers so you can refer to them throughout your break.

Fill in the blanks:

- The purpose of my career break is: _____.
- Ideally, I want to use it to: _____.
- In general, what I want to accomplish during my career break is:

  _____.

- During my time off, I want to make sure to: _____.
- I will know if my break has been effective or successful for me if:

  _____.

- When I look back on my break and if I were to describe it in five adjectives, they would be: _____.

Answer the following questions:

- How long will I take off—what is the range of time, minimum and maximum? (Make sure to factor in how much time you will need for a job search following your break.)

- What must I do to get my finances in order?
- What is my budget? How much do I need to live on while I'm out of work? What are my inflows (revenues) and outflows (expenses)? Can I cut back on expenses or make more money to build a nest egg if I need it? (For example, can I take on additional projects, more hours, etc. for a short time to make more money. To save on expenses, can I carpool, cut out my morning lattes and muffins, go out to eat 50 percent less per week than I do now, or do without my vacation or new car for this year?)
- What do I need to do now to ensure my break is a good one, not a disaster? (List what you need to do short-term, mid-term, and further out. For example, if you are thinking of a break in the future, you may need to save more money starting now, with the goal of building a nest egg of six months' cash reserve. For mid-term, after you have saved up your reserve and are taking your break, figure out how you'll tell people at work and transition your work and responsibilities smoothly. For longer term, you may look into a course or finding out about exploring a new industry or career change.)
- My worst fears about taking a break are that: _____. (For each fear, note at least two things you can do to eliminate or reduce that fear.)
- To be ready for reentry into my work or career, I want to start _____ months beforehand.
- I'll take these key steps to prepare during my break. For example, research MBA programs or two or three new industries or kinds of jobs; increase my circle of friends/network by X; get good hands-on experience (volunteer, project, or internship) in a media company; strengthen my teamwork and public speaking skills; increase my project management skills and leadership.

Six Ways to Keep Career-Fit While You're on Break

1. *Volunteer your services.* Take on a modest, low-stress, and minimal-time volunteer opportunity that uses your skills and strengths. For example,

be a graphics designer volunteer for the Humane Society's newsletter. A management consultant who is a whiz at PowerPoint presentations and spreadsheets could teach computers at an elementary school or to new immigrants.

2. *Find a creative new way to use your skills and strengths.* For example, a financial analyst helps his alma mater train new staff managers on "how to prepare a departmental budget" and suggests some new reports.

3. *Act as an informal adviser.* For example, a human resources recruiter offers tips and consultation to friends in many different industries on their hiring needs. A hairstylist offers to give "how to" make-up and hairstyling lessons for brides and their bridal parties. A board member for a nonprofit organization offers to serve as an informal adviser to its CEO on the most pressing challenges.

4. *Teach what you know.* The best way to learn often is to teach. Teach what it is you know and you increase your skills and knowledge, too. This will work well, particularly if you are changing careers and don't have actual experience in what you are hoping for. For example, teach through your city's Parks and Recreation or Community Services venues, network into your local community college or university, or host a program on your public access television station. Investigate local nonprofits that need expertise. Address a need for your church, synagogue, parish, or religious group. Perhaps it is teaching creative writing, job search skills, communication skills, or working in teams.

5. *Practice your skills daily.* In your daily life and activities, make a point to put to use the skills you are trying to keep up. If it's negotiation, try to negotiate something daily—the best price at a farmer's market, a discount on those car repairs, who gets to treat whom to lunch when you're out with your best friend. If it's organizational skills you are trying to maintain, incorporate them into whatever you are doing that day—doing a time and action plan for a house remodel, helping organize the volunteers for the community clean-up day, planning a multi-family garage sale or big birthday party. An example is a financial adviser who tries to beat the market daily by investing in his virtual portfolio at Market ocracy.com. Another is a Web designer who works on her own site regularly while on break and informally helps other friends and family with their personal or business-related Web sites.

6. *Serve on a board of directors or get involved in your community.* **Boards** for nonprofit and city government or public service organizations are always in need of bright, talented people who will share their experience and time. Go to your city's Web site and see what's new from the city manager's office. Perhaps she is convening a special group to review asset-driven revenue or a percent for art initiative. Contact your mayor or city council about your interest in serving your community. Look in your local newspaper about applications for commissions (Planning, Parks and Recreation, etc.,) or volunteer opportunities that may lead to board roles. Go to the Web site for BoardNetUSA—*www.boardnetusa.org/public/home*—to learn about board opportunities and to be matched with them.

Resequencing Your Career for Family

HAVE YOU BEEN a stay-at-home mom and are starting to think about how to jump back into a career? Has your wife put her career on hold to raise the kids and now you want to take some time off to be home while she resumes her career? Are you thinking of putting your family first and your career on the backburner for a while to spend more time with your family? Do you have a seriously ill parent you want to be there for and are willing to let your career take a backseat for as long as he or she needs you? What can you do to make it easier for your parent when you return to work? Did your husband recently take on more responsibility with a big promotion at work? How can you be there for him, manage the household, and be an active "corporate spouse"? If your wife has gotten the big promotion, what can you do to ease her transition, reduce her stress, and still maintain your own career?

● DEFINING THE CHALLENGE

If any of these situations hit home, read on. By resequencing, I mean rearranging your career to making your family the top priority. The typical scenario is to work hard to build a career before you have kids, step out of your career and take a break to focus on kids and family, then return to the workforce when you are ready. Resequencing is when you take time off expressly for family. You may be taking a break from your career to have a baby, raise your kids, take care of a sick parent or loved one, or just spend more time with or do more for your family. While this is still predominantly an issue that impacts women, more and more men recognize the value in and/or need for resequencing their careers.

The recent media stories about people who have put their careers on the backburner and their families first have highlighted the extreme difficulty people face when they attempt to return to the workforce. The stories discuss the bias on the part of recruiters, the deterioration of skills, and the inability for even extraordinary volunteer work to count for real, valued work experience. Still, there are many people—men and women—who have taken time off from their careers to put their families first, who are coming back into the world of work stronger, better, and more sure of what they do and don't want in their work lives.

● FACING THE CHALLENGE

If you have been fortunate enough to have the financial resources to choose to be a stay-at-home mom or dad, then you know that on most days you have no regrets. You feel that your decision was the right one. You wouldn't give back the time and experiences you have shared with your family. Now, fast forward to the time when you are starting to feel the lack of professional identity, the longing for something more in your life, and the sense that you want to be using your talents in a work situation with stimulating colleagues.

This is the "what's next" conundrum. You are at the stage in your life when you are asking some important questions that don't have quick, easy answers:

- What will I do with the rest of my life now that I've done what I wanted to for family?
- What is it like to think about me as a focus for a while?
- How can I step back into some sort of productive career?
- What is it that I want to do?
- The world of work has changed so much since I have been out of it. What am I capable of being hired for, of doing, of being paid for?
- How can I do work in context of my total life vision?

In my experience designing and directing Human Resources programs and policies to reintegrate women and men who had taken time off for their families, the journey back to work does not have to be one huge struggle. Realistically, stepping back into a career can be difficult, frustrating, and stressful, with closed doors, unimpressed recruiters, setbacks, and dead ends. You may have to take some steps backwards before moving forward. You can, however, step into the world of work and be happy, fulfilled, and satisfied. Read on and good luck!

Succeeding on Your Own Terms

Redefine "career." Realize that a career does not have to be a straight-line progression or a race to the top of a pyramid. Just because you can do something—for example, you have the talent to be a senior executive—does not mean that you should do it. Modern careers are more about conscious choices—making decisions that are good for you, the lifestyle you want, and what gives you meaning and purpose.

Careers for our times are more fluid, amorphous, and free-form than those in an earlier era. Back then, people typically went to work for one employer and remained there until they retired. Many married women stayed at home while their husbands worked. For our generation and those younger, careers look like a portfolio of diversified investments. Over a lifetime, you invest your time, energy, and talents in different jobs, multiple careers, and for a specific company/employer or work for yourself. The most fulfilling career is one that you define for yourself. It is on your terms and meets your expectations, not those of others. Consider how you would answer the following questions:

- What does true success mean?
- What do you want to achieve in your work life?
- What are your priorities?
- What is meaningful and purposeful for you?

Make sure to keep in career shape. There are things you can do while you are taking time off to ensure successful reentry into work. Your time away from your career for your family is not a time to let yourself go. You want to stay career-fit. If you are out of shape right now, then make some effort to get into shape. Take a look at the previous chapter on taking a career break.

Dedicate time for self-improvement. Work on improving your skills and strengths. Use this opportunity-rich time to engage your skills and keep yourself intellectually stimulated. During the time you are off, maintain a great circle of friends, including some you knew in your work life. When you're ready to go back to work, they are the first contacts to call upon for your networking. Make some quiet time for yourself to reflect on the bigger picture—your life vision and how work and career fit into that. Ponder questions, if you don't already know the answers, such as, What is your purpose? What are your passions?

Plan ahead. At least six months to a year before you expect to be going back to work, read or reread the chapters on doing a job search, creating a strong résumé, learning to interview well, values-based decision making for your job search, and making a major career change. When generating options for what you want to do next, make sure they fit realistically with what you can do within a reasonable stretch. Reach high, but keep your feet on the ground. If there is something you have always dreamed about, figure out the sequence steps and milestones to take to get there.

Bring yourself up to date. If you want to get back into your industry and you have been out for 5, 10, or even 15 years, make sure you are up to date on the lingo, the vibe (energy and style), the trends, the challenges, the key players, and what is happening in the industry. Study everything you can to "get smart" again on the industry. Tap into all the best resources you know. These include former colleagues and managers, a professional association or special interests groups, periodicals and journals, Web sites, and the like.

A priceless resource is someone who is an expert immersed in the industry. Ask him to spend 30 minutes with you over coffee or on the telephone. Pepper the person with lots of questions and ask for advice and insights on your reentry. Find out where the jobs are and what they are. What companies are hiring? What are the qualifications and where do you have some shortcomings to fill in? Consider taking an individual-contributor role that is a few levels below where you were when you left. This would allow more flexibility in schedule and less stress, and it would give you the leeway to retool your experience and resharpen your skills. If you want to leapfrog ahead after you're back in the swing of things, then you can do that.

Reinventing Your Career

Dip your toes in the water. Chances are that while you were away from your career, you decided that when you did return to work, you would make a change. Identify the two or three kinds of jobs you want to try. Start small by taking on projects, apprenticing, or interning in a role similar to what you want to move into. Build up some relevant and marketable experience. Don't worry for now about being paid. Work experience is work experience. Consider that your compensation is the experience and references that you are cultivating. What you choose to take on should also focus on building some substance in the new career for your résumé. Creating some current, tangible experience in the career you are trying for will make a difference when you apply and interview for jobs.

Change careers. Take a look at Chapter 17 on making a major career change. It is filled with good ideas and advice. Explore various avenues for getting yourself involved in the new field. For example, if you have been in public relations but now want to do something art related, you could take on some part-time projects with a museum that draw on your PR and communication talents. There are many ways to get your foot in the door:

- Volunteer for arts-related organizations in your community. Your city's Web site, local Chamber of Commerce, or newspaper's "volunteers needed" section are helpful resources.
- Familiarize yourself with the museum or organization you are interested in by taking a look at its Web site and/or reviewing its annual report.
- Contact the director of Development or Corporate Relations to express your interest.
- Network through someone you know already on the board or affiliated with the organization.

- Work on the annual report, the invitations and press releases for a big fund-raising event, the communication strategy for a capital campaign or a new exhibit.
- See if you can serve on the Board of Directors. Your board work will put you in contact with the senior managers running the organization. You will learn about the more strategic issues and challenges. You'll get to know the inner workings of the operation.

Wiggle your way in. If you have a list of targeted organizations or industries and kinds of jobs you want to work in, ask for specific help from your friends and family. Find people in your past or present who can refer you or help you get closer to the job or company you want. For example, talk with other parents you have been volunteering with at your child's school. They have spouses or partners who work or have companies they work for themselves. Another approach is to reconnect with the staff that you mentored and developed when you were working. Most have probably continued to do well and are in a position to hire you now! Your former boss who thought you walked on water is also probably still going strong somewhere or would be willing to refer you to others like her who are hiring.

Start at the bottom. If you want to break into a new field, sometimes to be able to get a full-time job again you may have to start at the bottom. Rather than look at it as an embarrassment or a setback, view it as a learning experience. If you shine and perform well, chances are you will move up quickly.

Be a trainee. Be willing to start in the trainee program, serve as a PA (personal assistant doing administrative work) for someone with big responsibility, or work in a job at a lower level than when you stepped out of your career. If that's what it takes and you want to make a move into this new arena, then do it. Do it with the knowledge that you will work your way back up. You need to build a new track record of performance before advancing. The benefit is that you are establishing a strong foundation of learning, new skills and experience, and valuable relationships. You will be well versed and knowledgeable about the day-to-day responsibilities of your new career.

Think about the future. You may not want to be in this next career forever. Most likely you'll have a few more jobs or careers left in you before you retire. Enjoy what you are doing and learn all you can, but be thinking about and leisurely exploring what you'll do next in your career. Think of your career as designing a beautiful and vibrant mosaic with many colors and patterns that all fit together.

● Tools and Resources

A Personalized Questionnaire

When you feel the urge to think about returning to your career or some kind of work outside the home, reflect on the following questions. Write down your answers in a journal, in a notebook, or on your computer for future reference. Take a few questions each time so that you can set aside 30 minutes or so until you have answered all of these. What you decide, your preferences and priorities, will provide good guidance as you begin to develop your reentry strategy and plan.

- Reflect on the time you worked outside the home. What did you like most about your jobs or roles? What strengths, skills, and abilities did you enjoy using the most? What was it about the people— your manager, your peers, those who reported to you—that inspired, motivated, or made you feel rewarded?
- During your time away from your career, what have you learned about yourself?
- Think about what you want now as you gear up to return to some kind of career or work. What are your priorities, your career goals and objectives? What kind of schedule is ideal? How many hours a week do you really want to be working?
- What is your current financial situation? Can you afford to take a job you love even if it does not pay well or do you need to earn a good income to support the family?

- You've probably already achieved a lot. What more is left that you want to do, be, or become in your life? What are your aspirations outside of your family?
- What kinds of work, jobs, and careers fit with what you want to continue to do with and for your family?
- Identify three small steps you can take sometime between now and next month to explore these kinds of work, jobs, and careers that are a fit.
- Once you've taken those three steps, identify the next three steps you need to take and do them. Keep chipping away at the successive steps you need to take to move you closer to the next job/career you want.
- What does your partner or spouse think about your returning to work? How will this impact your family? How will you work it out so the transition back to work, whether full-time, part-time, or project-based (episodic), is as smooth as possible.
- What are you most frightened or intimidated by about going back to work? For example, many resequencers fear rejection; possessing outdated skills and knowledge; or not fitting in, such as working with much younger people, lots of MBAs, or managers who may be 10 years their junior.
- After acknowledging what you may be fearful or intimidated about, think about what you can do to combat each of these fears.

Take a look at the useful Web sites listed in Chapters 1, 16, and 17. Here are some others:

Some Useful Web Sites

- *Fast Company* Magazine—*www.fastcompany.com/articles/*. Review the categories Personal Growth and Development, specifically the sections "Launch Your Career," "Reinvent Yourself," "Job Titles of the Future," and "Go Solo."
- Monster.com—*www.monster.com*. Touts more than 1 million job postings. Can be used to research companies, search for job listings, and find out your market value through a "personal salary report."

Includes a global network of experts and resources. There is also information and help for self-employment or contract or temporary work.

- *Working Mother/Working Woman* Magazine—*www.workingwoman.com*. Check out the annual list of "100 Best Companies for Working Mothers."
- Advancing Women—*www.advancingwomen.com*. International business career community for women in the workplace.
- National Association for Female Executives—*www.nafe.com*. Empowering women with the tools and resources to become successful entrepreneurs and business owners.
- Women Work—*www.wwork.com*. Resources that help people move from corporations to smaller firms or to setting up their own business.
- Catalyst—*www.catalystwomen.org*. Nonprofit dedicated to advancing women in business. Research, tips, and career advice for women.

Trailing Your Spouse or Partner to a New Location

HAS YOUR HUSBAND recently gotten a promotion and you are moving to a new city? Has your partner accepted an international assignment in a different country? Has your wife received a plumb new job that will require you and your kids to move cross-country? Are you in a serious long-distance relationship and thinking about moving to be closer to your significant other (SO)?

● DEFINING THE CHALLENGE

When you're the trailing spouse, partner, or SO, following your loved one to another city or even a new country for him or her to accept a job or promotion can be extremely stressful. Even if you had the ideal circumstances—you were in on the discussion, part of the decision, and supportive of the move—it means upsetting important dimensions of your life. Being a trailing partner or spouse can be a problem because it can mean leaving behind family and friends and a job and colleagues you enjoy, giving up a hard-earned salary, or saying goodbye to "sweat equity" in a company or industry where you are known and have a track record.

If your industry is highly specialized, your hiatus from it could make you less competitive when you return, since your skills could become outdated. Also, for some companies and industries, the old saying "out of sight, out of mind" often holds true. If you're not around, they could forget you. And in this job market, there are many other talented people who would like to take your place.

● FACING THE CHALLENGE

Trailing your spouse or partner probably means you have to start from scratch. First, you have to find a new job if you plan to work. You have to learn your new environment and culture, build your reputation, and make new business contacts. If there are specialized laws, business practices, or experience required for working in your new home city or country, all of this will put you back at square one.

The problem of trailing a spouse can be exasperating because typically the person doing the following will not have the security of a job offer in hand for the new place or the instant support or camaraderie of company colleagues. Your partner, even if super supportive, will be busy starting his or her new job. Additionally, since the trailing partner doesn't have a job to jump into right away, this person will end up with the lion's share of responsibility for handling the details of the move, including the setup of a new household.

Trailing a spouse really can be bleak if you focus on all of the negatives. The "problem" also can be an enormous opportunity, a fresh start, and an incredible learning and growth experience if you can make it so. Read on.

Do a Reality Check

Think about and plan your move as best you can. Sit down and discuss with your partner how you can make the best possible situation for both of you. Some questions or factors to consider are:

- What do each of you need now from the other in terms of support, decisions made, information, or communication?
- How much time do you need to make the move? The company may require your partner to start the new job right away, but is it critical that you leave urgently, too?
- How much time do you want to give notice to your current employer? Will you want to help find and transition a successor?
- What do you need to do with your current house or apartment?
- How will you go about finding a new place in your new city?
- How best can you check out schools for your children?

- What requirements are there, such as vaccinations and quarantining, for moving your pets with you?

Making It Work

Think about staying behind for a while. If the time is too short, putting undue pressure on you, consider having your partner go ahead while you stay behind for a time. Take the time to handle what you need to in a way that empowers you and gives you some control over your situation. Your partner can live in temporary housing. You can plan periodic trips to the new location to house or apartment hunt while acclimating to your new environment in small doses.

Take some fear out of the unknown. Research your new home city or country. By taking the bull by the horns and learning about the new place, you will empower yourself with knowledge. When you have clearer perspective on where you are going, what you're getting into, and what to expect, you can then plan to deal with it. If you don't know, usually the fear of it is worse than the reality. Actively discovering more about your new home will also generate some excitement for your move. Set your mind to viewing it as an adventure, a chance to learn and explore new experiences, and a positive growth opportunity for you and your partner.

There are several excellent sources for researching your new environs. Start at the library. Ask the reference librarian to guide you to books or videos that will give you a feel and background information for your new city or country. Use Internet search engines such as Google or Yahoo! to do research on your new home place. Make a point of reading a local paper online periodically to gain perspective on current events, politics, education, arts and entertainment, and personalities and people. Ask around in your circle of friends and family. Find a few people—in situations similar to yours if possible—who have lived or who are living in your new city. Talk with them for advice on possible pitfalls, what to make sure to do, and what not to do.

Consider not working. If you can afford not to work, think about taking a break for a while. For example, give yourself a sabbatical to rejuvenate, learn a new culture, or pursue a passion. This is a good time to consider a career break and to reap all of its benefits! Assess your financial situation. What do you need to live on? Will your working spouse or partner make enough money for your needs and savings and investment goals?

Create a shared vision. Collaborate with your spouse on what you want your individual and shared experience in the new city to look like, feel like, be like. Spend some time envisioning and discussing what a great experience for the both of you would look and feel like. What will it include? How will it be different from what you have together now? When you reflect on your time in the new place, what will you want to have accomplished? How would you like to describe this time in your life when looking back on it? An exercise to create an ideal vision of what you want your experience to be like is included in the last section of this chapter.

Put a job search on hold for now. If you think you'd like to work in the new city, take a look at Chapters 1 and 17 on doing a job search and making a major career change to keep in mind what you'll need to do later on. Don't worry about starting on a job search until you have moved and are in your new home. You will need time to settle in, then focus on your job search.

Do something if you must. If you are anxious about finding a new job and you would feel better doing something now, then by all means, go ahead. Do some light research and exploration on promising sectors and organizations for your new location. Spend time on your self-marketing, thinking of your 5 P's (see Chapter 1, Figure 1-1). Train or airplane travel to and from your current and new locations is ideal for meaningful reflection and progress on job search activities. While you don't want to over-stress yourself trying to do too much before your move, if you can swing it, accomplish a few activities in familiar environs to make your job search easier in the long run. Completing some key elements will give you a springboard for when you move to your new location.

Get a quick take on the culture and the customs. For a job search in a different city that is highly dissimilar to where you are now, take some extra time to investigate the history of the new place, the culture, the people, customs, business norms, and so on. Quick sources of valuable information are people who have worked there who you can talk to or e-mail, or a local business journal or newspaper you can read online or at your local library. Some of my favorite resources before we moved to London for a few years because of my husband's work were Stanford alumni living in London who were willing to share their insights, work colleagues who knew people who had lived there or were from there, and watching some London-based programs on the telly.

Incorporate settling-in time. Give yourself six to eight weeks to get settled in before going full throttle on your job search. You'll need ample time to find a place to live; get your computers, Internet connection, telephone, and fax machine set up; start up your services like electricity, water, and trash; figure out the transportation system; identify where you'll shop for food and clothes; choose a gym, cleaners, and shoe repair shop; find out where you can get things photocopied, have pictures developed, find a good travel agent, and other such matters.

Establish some lifelines. Figure out ways to get the emotional support and encouragement you need. Give your friends, family, and work colleagues your new contact information as soon as you have it. Invite them to visit. Set up your instant messaging (IM—real-time conversations involving messages typed to another or with a group on the computer) account and ask your friends and family to establish accounts, too, so you can IM back and forth. Sign up for a telephone service that allows inexpensive calling to your friends and family back home. Consider establishing a regular call time to talk each week for your best friend, your parents, or other close family members.

Career Transition Assistance

Use your spouse's career transition services. Find out what career transition services the company offers trailing spouses or partners. Set up a meeting or telephone call with the person in your spouse's company who will be handling your move. Ask what services they provide for the relocation. Most companies are generous in their relocation in terms of housing, cars, cost of living adjustments, and the like.

Sometimes the company will also offer help to the trailing spouse in areas such as continuing professional development. This could include financial support for you to attend career conferences, dues for professional association memberships or journal subscriptions, or the cost of classes related to your profession or for your job search in your new location. Sometimes, the company will connect you with a career counselor or job placement firm for your new location. These professionals can help you craft a job search, customize your CV/résumé, and prepare for interviewing. They can familiarize you with the recruiting customs and norms and give you a briefing on the job market and hiring process. The most effective ones will also provide you with actual job leads or opportunities.

Create your own transition services. If the company doesn't offer career transition resources, it might be willing to do something informally if you ask. It already thinks highly of your spouse and needs him or her in the new location. This move is a big investment and a successful transition is one in which the trailing spouse and family members are happy, supportive, and taken care of. Pragmatically speaking, distractions or frustrations must be minimized for your partner, who needs to jump into the new job. It is a smart business decision for a company to offer help for the trailing spouse. If it doesn't, often it's not because it doesn't want to. Perhaps, the company hasn't had to in the past; doesn't have the money, staff or know-how; or just hasn't thought to do it because the practice is so new.

Ask and you could receive. Take the burden off of your spouse's company and proactively convey the specific help, within reason, that you would appreciate. The company might not be able to do everything you ask for, but something is better than nothing at all. The career transition resources noted above are a good basis for what to request. Additionally, asking to be assigned a host family in your new city is not unreasonable and is something fairly easy for the company to do. Ideally, this would be a family who has lived there a while or perhaps all of their lives. The host family could serve as informal mentors, answer your questions, big or small, and help you acclimate quickly to daily living in your new environment. They may also be a viable source for job contacts or leads.

Call on your network. In any job search, calling on a diverse circle of family, friends, and contacts is useful. Contact your university or graduate school and ask for a listing of alumni in your new city. Make sure to get e-mail addresses and/or telephone numbers. When letting your family, friends, and work colleagues know that you are moving and providing your new contact details, ask them for referrals to their friends, family, and colleagues who are in the new location. If you know you will conduct a job search, let your network know which areas (industry, or type of organization or job) you want to consider.

Get a sense of the market. Choose a few select Internet job listing sites and get a sense of the job market in the new place. Who is hiring? What's the pay like? What skills and experience are in demand? Check out what career services assistance is available once you get there—a sister school's career services office, professional or social groups that offer job leads or support, and the best sources to find the job opportunities. These could include newspapers, church or religious groups' bulletin boards, your new neighborhood or gym's newsletters, chamber of commerce–like organizations, employment agencies, and organizations that have affiliates around the world, such as the American Association of University Women, International Federation of University Women, or Rotary International.

Consider telecommuting. Think about telecommuting or project work or consulting jobs with your current employer. If you absolutely love your job and cannot bear the thought of leaving it, then be creative! Initiate discussions with your boss, a well-placed mentor, Human Resources, or someone else empathetic in your current organization. Ask about a creative way to continue working in the company but from a "remote" location. Many jobs lend themselves to this sort of telecommuting. Basically any work you can do that is transportable and does not require a lot of daily, face-to-face interaction with colleagues is a good possibility.

Sometimes your particular job cannot be done from somewhere else but you have the skills to do something else for your employer that can be done from your new location. Examples are writing or editing (internal communications, annual reports or company or recruiting brochures, executive team or CEO speeches), research and analysis, putting together a marketing strategy or PR campaign, handling media requests, or developing training materials for a new program. Serving as a consultant to a group or on specific projects is another possibility—for example, consulting on a post-merger plan, a new human resources information system, competitive research for the strategic plan of a new division, or a new initiative in accounting or finance. Reporting and analysis are discrete activities that can be performed off-site.

Ask for a transfer within your company. If your company has a subsidiary, division, or branch office in the new city, ask for a transfer. Find the person or people who can help you learn about the opportunities. Enlist the person's help in facilitating or championing interviews or arranging for a transfer. If you've had a good track record in your organization, possess valuable skills and experience, and are well regarded within your company, a transfer is very viable.

Don't become obsolete. Keep up your skills. Whether formally in a job or now at your new location, continue to develop your skills and knowledge for your field and industry. Purchase an online subscription to your industry journal. Arrange for a few colleagues to formally touch base with you via bi-monthly IM sessions. Ask that they keep you abreast of what's going on in your company and with the industry. If IM is too much to ask of them, request that they forward to you company e-mails or articles that keep you in the know. Volunteer in your new home city or country so you use your skills and talents regularly. Refer to Chapter 18 on taking a career break for other ideas and advice.

● TOOLS AND RESOURCES

Creating a Shared Vision

Try this brief exercise. It is designed to get you discussing your individual and as-a-couple needs and wants about the move, however you envision it. By identifying each other's point of view, you can better know how to support each other as well as pinpoint where there might be conflicts that need discussion and resolution.

- Set aside about an hour to meet someplace that you both like and feel relaxed in. It could be your family room, by the pool, on your favorite park bench, or at a café.
- Before you meet, each of you should think about the following three statements and jot down your thoughts on a piece of paper.
  1. When we look back on this experience, I'd be happy if during the time there we: _____.
  2. The five adjectives that describe the experience I want to have in our new home are: _____.
  3. I want the experience in our new city to be different from what we have now in these ways: _____.
- Bring these answers with you when you meet. Swap answers with each other.
- For the first 10 minutes, read aloud each other's answers. Your spouse or partner will read from your answers as though he or she were you. You will read from your spouse or partner's answers as though you were him or her.
- Take back your own answers and linger on each item, explaining what you meant by your answer.

Customizing Your Job Search Action Plan

Refer to Chapter 1 on doing a job search for specific ideas on how to develop a job search action plan. For your homework before you start on your job search action plan for your new location, conduct some research on your new environs. Address the questions outlined below:

- What's the economic climate like?
- What industries and sectors are strong and/or growing?
- Which are the reputable companies and organizations (such as universities or the office of tourism)?
- What are the cultural norms that I need to know to do well there?

- How are the people there different from where I live now?
- How are they similar?
- What will I need to be culturally sensitive to, especially in how they do business, how they communicate, and how they handle conflict, disagreement, or negotiation?
- What would be a major faux pas—a big mistake—in the new culture?
- How can I find out about the recruiting and hiring processes there—particularly how people learn about jobs, the interviewing norms, negotiating dos and don'ts, etc.?
- What can I do now, before we've moved, to get me off to a good start? For example, can I begin to customize my résumé? Can I gather contact names and how to reach them for networking later?
- If I cannot get the clearance to work in the country (assuming a move to a new country in which you do not have citizenship and there are stringent limitations on work permits), what volunteer opportunities will help keep me stimulated and my skills current?
- How will I have to repackage or reposition my experience and strengths to best fit my new location?

Sources to help you with the answers include your spouse's relocation services counselor in the new location; alumni from your graduate or undergraduate program in the new location; select Internet resources (do a keyword search on Google or Yahoo!); your network referrals from family, friends, and work colleagues; selected books from your local library; and newspapers from your new home place. If your time and patience are limited, ask an executive recruiter friend to put you in touch with a colleague in your new location. These professionals are so knowledgeable that even 30 minutes on the phone will give you a valuable overview.

Some Internet Resources for Preparing for Your Move

- BestPlaces.net—*www.bestplaces.net*. Lists best places to live. Includes links to other surveys. Provides city profiles and comparisons. Covers schools, crime, and climate profiles.
- Monster.com Relocation Coordinator—*www.monstermoving.com*. A helpful source for your move. Offers information on movers, mort-

gage rates, storage facilities, utilities, a good move planner, and free address changing.

- Relocation Central—*www.relocationcentral.com*. Links to real estate, health care, and Chamber of Commerce resources.
- Newcomers Club—*wwwnewcomersclub.com*. A worldwide directory of clubs and organizations that welcome you into town.
- VolunteerMatch—*volunteermatch.org*. This is a service that takes into consideration your individual interests and matches you with local volunteer opportunities in your new area.
- The American Association of University Women—*www.aauw.org*. This organization has chapters across the United States and internationally. Activities include book, movie, and dining groups.
- Organizations to try if you are a mother—*mothersandmore.org, mops.org, motherscenter.org*.

Not Being Sure of Your Purpose and Path

ARE YOU GOOD at what you do but don't feel fulfilled or satisfied with your career? Do you have a sense that there is something more out there for you workwise? Do you know in your heart that you are not doing what you were born to do? You know you have a calling, but you just haven't figured out exactly what that is. Do you wake up most mornings uninspired about going to work? Does your job make you feel like you are a fish out of water? Do you yearn to do something that you have always loved, but you think it's not serious enough to make a living from? Is there a certain kind of job you have a strong interest in, but landing it would be against all odds? Do you ever feel like you are watching a movie on your life but you are not in it? Do you see yourself going through the motions of your career but it's not the real you?

● DEFINING THE CHALLENGE

If any of these scenarios sound familiar, it could be that you are unsure about your career purpose and path. Some people know their purpose in life early on—their calling, their destiny, what they were born to do. Perhaps as young as childhood, one just knows he or she was born to be an actor, a doctor, a teacher, an entrepreneur, in public service, a professional athlete, or a CEO. For others, figuring out their purpose and path may come much later. They have to cycle through a few jobs or careers. Perhaps it comes as the result of an epiphany, a mid-life or quarter-life crisis, a watershed event like a life-threatening illness, a death in the family, being fired, or a spiritual awakening. Not being sure of your purpose and path is a challenge that most of us encounter at some point in our work lives.

● FACING THE CHALLENGE

How do you know if you are unsure of your career purpose and path, or at least not following them? Although there's no easy fix, no quick answers, no magic pill to reveal your purpose and path, this chapter can guide you through some crucial foundational steps to get you on your way. The chapter provides insights about how you may recognize your purpose, why you have been avoiding it, and how to remove those restraints. You are provided with advice and exercises on how to gain clarity about what your purpose and path really are. You are encouraged, and we hope inspired, to let your purpose keep trying to find you until you let it!

Rather than a lot of to-do's and answers, this chapter is mostly about reflecting, being aware, asking yourself questions, and knowing when to follow the signals and clues toward the amorphous, touchy-feely life forces that are your purpose and path.

Go Back to Your Roots

Express yourself. There are many reasons you are not living your career purpose just yet. You need to identify what's holding you back. Allow yourself to express what you think your purpose may be. As a start, do any of these sound familiar to your situation?

- Perhaps you haven't realized until recently that you want or deserve something more from your career. Maybe you have been too busy achieving, buying your financial freedom, or making ends meet to stop and think about this higher order stuff.
- Maybe you don't want to let others down. Your parents or spouse have certain expectations of you and your lifestyle. They have set your bar—the standard or definition of what you should do and be. And you have complied.
- Perhaps you have felt your calling for a long time but have side-

stepped it. You have a fear of failure or rejection, are too invested in your current career to give that up, or think your true purpose seems frivolous to pursue given your education and background.

- Perhaps your next job has always just found you. You have always been recruited, pursued, or somehow "fell" into your career. It's been nice to sit back and let that happen.

Whatever the reasons for not being sure of or pursuing your career path, face them, let them go, then start the journey to finding your purpose.

Ponder it. Take a look at the exercises, tools, and resources at the end of this chapter. These will guide you through some of the important questions to help you clarify your purpose. Remember that a purpose can be something as beautifully simple as to make a positive difference in others' lives, to teach others, to build a great company, to help bring about world peace, to be a loving parent, or to help eradicate poverty and hunger. For example:

- Why are you here on earth?
- What is your reason for being?
- What motivates you?
- What is meaningful to you?
- When you are at the end of your life, what do you want to look back on and see that you've achieved?

Be a child. Think back to when you were a child. What did you dream of becoming? What did you want to be when you grew up? Now that you are grown up, does this still appeal to you?

For Love and Money

Make like a millionaire. Envision yourself as if you woke up one morning and had won a $10 million lottery. Money is no longer a constraint. What would you choose to be doing?

Do what you love and the money will follow. There is a healthy debate from career experts about following your passion and doing what you love.

One school of thought is that if you do what you love, you'll starve. Some career experts will contend that your job or career *is* for the money. It's for the paycheck. You don't rely on your job for meaning and enjoyment. Those things you look for outside of your work.

I am and have always been a strong believer in encouraging people to follow their passions and let the money follow. My experiences have shown that those who do what they love in their work are happier overall, more fulfilled in their careers, and usually more productive. If each of us is spending the majority of our time awake working, then shouldn't it be something that we love to do and with people whom we enjoy? After all, life is too short.

Take your skills in a new direction. While your specific job and career may no longer appeal to you, you may be able to incorporate your skills and experience into following your purpose and path. If you are good at what you do, you probably enjoy it on some level. Perhaps over the years you have lost sight of or never found your true career purpose, so you continue to blindly apply your abilities to the wrong area. Once you identify your true career path, many times you'll be able to fully apply your existing skills to a task you were born to follow. This can create a beautiful harmony in both your career and your life.

Experiment and see what sticks. Try some different things workwise and see what sticks. If you think being a sports agent, a banker, a teacher, a personal trainer, an entrepreneur, an actor, or a consultant is your calling, then find or create work opportunities to try it. That could be within your current career, profession, or industry or could mean making a big career change. Refer to Chapters 1 and 17 on doing a job search and making a major career change.

For example, maybe you have been a management consultant for a top strategy firm, but you think your calling is helping less fortunate people who are in war-torn countries to have a better life. You may ask your firm to assign you some pro bono projects for some nonprofit organizations that have similar missions and purposes. Later on you may start your own consulting firm to nonprofits or find work with the Red Cross, Doctors Without Borders, the Peace Corps, or a relief organization.

Be aware. Often your purpose and path will find you if you let them. Perhaps out of the blue you are offered a once-in-a-lifetime opportunity. You are happily going along in your career and then bang–someone from your past, a new acquaintance, someone you have admired from afar–finds you and invites you to do something. Maybe you keep running into someone who is trying to recruit you to work for him. Perhaps you keep feeling a strong pull toward a specific new field.

Take measured risk. Of course, you will need to assess the risk, be realistic about what you can do given your financial situation, and get career advice from those you trust. I'd say trust your instincts, and if you know something has been presented to you that will take you one step closer to living your purpose and path, then do it. If it turns out to be a mulligan, as they say in golf, then take another shot. At most, you will have lost a few months and you will have some interesting new experience to boot.

● TOOLS AND RESOURCES

Jim Collins, one of my favorite professors at the Stanford Graduate School of Business, is coauthor of the bestseller *Built to Last: Successful Habits of Visionary Companies* (HarperBusiness) and author of *Good to Great: Why Some Companies Make the Leap . . . and Others Don't* (HarperBusiness). Jim challenged us as students to do an exercise in his class that made an imprint on my heart. His wisdom sparked many of us to embark on a journey that would transform our work lives.

Jim suggests finding the intersection among three interlocking circles: (1) What are my purpose and passions in life and what do I stand for? (2) What am I good at–genetically encoded for; what would I be doing if I felt like a fish *in* water? (3) What makes economic and financial sense for me? What can I make a living from? See Figure 21-1.

Take a look at the three interlocking circles. Ask yourself the questions for each circle.

Jot down ideas for each circle. Where's the intersection? Think about and research the kinds of work and a career that will enable

Figure 21-1. Jm Collins's Purpose and Path Exercise

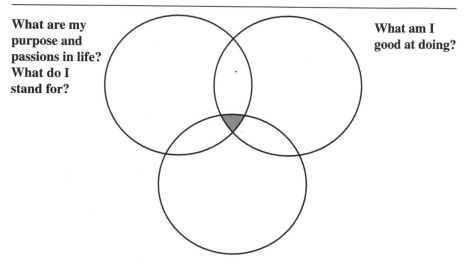

What are my purpose and passions in life? What do I stand for?

What am I good at doing?

What makes economic and financial sense for me? How can I make a living from doing what I live and am good at?

you to tap into the intersection of doing what you love, are good at, and can make a living from.

What's My Line?

What's your line—your higher purpose, your reason for being in the universe? Picture yourself on a bare stage with an audience who entreats you to tell them: What's your line? Read over the sentences below. Set aside 20 minutes to reflect on how you would fill in the blanks. Write your completed sentences somewhere so you can refer to them later. At another time, set aside one hour. Bring your filled-in purpose statements with you. Make a list of 10 ways your purpose would or could be realized.

Part I: Choose one sentence from these five. Fill in the blank.

1. Deep down, I know I was born to

_____ .

2. The reason I am here on earth is to

_____.

3. My mission in life is

_____.

4. My reason for being is

_____.

5. If I died tomorrow, I would want to have made sure to have

_____.

Part II: Based on your purpose statement, make a Top Ten list of ways your purpose would or could be realized. For example, suppose one of your purpose statements was "The reason I am here on earth is to teach, help, and inspire others." Your Top Ten list might include:

1. "I want to try for work that incorporates three objectives: to teach, help, and inspire others, especially adults as related to their careers."

2. "There are many arenas that allow me to teach, help, and inspire. The ones most stimulating and fulfilling to me are writing, speaking, and career advising."

3. "For me to live my purpose, I also want to integrate my values: being creative, being passionate about what I do, and making a positive difference in peoples' lives."

Write Your Own Obituary

Find some quiet, comfortable place to do this exercise. Bring your laptop or a pad of paper and a pen. Write your own obituary in 250 words or less. Make sure to give it a headline and include as vivid of a description as possible of how people will remember you. What did you stand for in your life? What did you accomplish? What legacy did you leave for future generations and your family?

Index